GREEN LIGHT MILLIONAIRE

How Ordinary People Build Wealth
Using the Stoplight Strategy

GREEN LIGHT MILLIONAIRE

DAVE DEVRIES

CFP®, CKA®, RICP®, MDIV

ENDORSEMENTS

I know from many years of giving financial counsel that all behavior is a function of a belief system, and your belief system comes from what you know and think. Dave has written a book which will both challenge and/or encourage your thinking and consequently your financial decision-making. He has presented the truth in a rational, logical, and compelling way and I recommend this book highly for anyone who wants to change or know whether they are thinking right when it comes to money and money management.

– Ron Blue,
Founder of Kingdom Advisors,
National Christian Foundation and Blue Trust

Dave does a wonderful job of breaking down complex financial concepts into simple, easy-to-understand illustrations, such as his green and red light examples. It reminds me of classics like The Millionaire Next Door *and* Rich Dad Poor Dad, *but Dave adds a unique touch by drawing from his Midwest values and Christian background to bring the lessons to life. Whether you're just starting your career or approaching retirement, this book offers valuable insights that can benefit anyone.*

– Scott Carlson,
Regional Vice President, Osaic Wealth

Green Light Millionaire *is a clear, practical, and inspiring guide to wealth development done the right way. Dave connects biblical principles with everyday financial decisions in a way that builds both your financial wealth and your financial wisdom. This isn't just about getting rich, it's about growing wiser and creating a legacy that lasts. Every Christian who wants to honor God with their finances should read this book.*

– Bob Merritt,
Founder of Eagle Brook Church in Minneapolis, St. Paul;
author, speaker, leadership coach

Dave is someone whose wisdom and advice I trust. The same can be said about Green Light Millionaire. *Dave's words and real life examples ring true, and offer so much wisdom, not just on finances, but also on simply being good stewards of what God has given us. Dave personally lives out every word. Whatever your current financial situation or future goals, I would highly recommend turning to this book for the incredible resource it is!*

– Adam Weber,
Lead Pastor of Embrace Church, author, podcast host

Green Light Millionaire *is packed with practical principles that help guide your path toward a financial future that matches your life goals and desires. If you are like me, (not a financial expert) this is an excellent resource that makes sense in terms we understand. I wish I had this book twenty-five years ago, but I'm gaining great fresh insights now and I'll make sure my kids get a copy!*

– Dan Reiland,
Leadership Coach, Church Strategist, https://danreiland.com

In Green Light Millionaire, *Dave distills wealth-building into something both practical and deeply personal. His stoplight strategy is more than financial advice—it's a mindset shift that helps you see every decision as a green light toward freedom or a red light holding you back. This book doesn't just tell you how to grow your net worth; it shows you how to grow a life you truly want.*

– Matt Jensen,
Principal & Founder at Mend Join Make - MJM

Dave has a gift for making financial principles simple, relatable, and actionable. What I appreciate most is that Dave lives out what he teaches—his Green Light Millionaire *approach isn't theory, it's proven and practical. I can confidently say his work will challenge how you think about money and give you a clear path toward lasting success*

– Todd Tryon,
Commissioner, Indoor Football League

Dave uses practical examples and biblical principles in his book illustrating how to build personal wealth. Timeless common sense strategies told through story and characters. I highly recommend making an investment of your time in this book.

– Doug Morrison,
Former CFO, Citibank

Green Light Millionaire *is a practical guide, based on solid biblical principles, for the reader to realize a brighter financial future. The Green Light - Red Light approach is one we can all identify with and provides a foundation for Dave to explain how all of us can realize our financial goals without sacrificing the joy that comes with living a life of faith. If you choose to invest in this book and embrace the principles outlined, your life will be better and "richer" because of it. This book makes the complex quite simple for all of us!*

– Rick Melmer,
Former Secretary of Education - SD, RVM Consulting

Green Light Millionaire *simplifies what so many people overcomplicate. It's not about chasing the perfect investment—it's about thinking differently, building the right habits, and aligning your money with what matters most. His stoplight analogy sticks with you and makes the path to financial freedom feel both doable and motivating.*

– Ryan Boen,
CFO, Cambridge Investment Research

Dave has created a simple yet powerful framework that makes understanding and managing money approachable for anyone. The stoplight analogy brings clarity to building wealth, while the biblical foundation anchors it in timeless truth. This is a must-read for anyone seeking financial wisdom with eternal perspective.

– Dr. Nathan Unruh,
President, FiveFour

This book is dedicated to all those who have become Green Light Millionaires and are now looking to pass that wealth and knowledge to the next generation. You have worked hard your whole life to be where you are today. May this book be a guide to help you in those conversations of how to build wealth and wisely steward those resources for generations to come. To the soon to be "Green Light Millionaires", may this book be a guide to help you on your financial journey. Yes, there will be roadblocks and detours. Stay focused on your goals and may you hit as many "Green Lights" as possible to help you achieve your goals.

Throne Publishing Group
ThronePG.com

TABLE OF CONTENTS

PREFACE

Why do the rich keep getting richer? Do they really have some magic formula that allows them to become millionaires? Before becoming a financial advisor and eventually a senior partner at a wealth management practice, I was a pastor for nine years and worked for nonprofits many years prior to that. I was always intrigued at building wealth even though my wife and I never had large incomes. As I worked with clients, I realized some individuals had large incomes but very little net worth. I also worked with clients who didn't have huge incomes, but had large amounts of net worth. I quickly realized what had the biggest impact on who was actually a millionaire at the end of the day: how each person/family thought about their finances.[1]

I was blessed to be mentored by some amazing people early on and adopted those financial principles for my household. We didn't win the lottery. We didn't sell off a business for a huge profit or get lucky on a single real estate deal. But, we consistently followed financial principles that have allowed us the freedom to do the things we dreamed

---

[1] This material is for general information and educational purposes only. Information is based on data gathered from what we believe are reliable sources. It is not guaranteed as to accuracy, does not purport to be complete and is not intended to be used as a primary basis for investment decisions.

of financially. Everyone wants to be successful, but very few want to do what successful people do that makes them successful.

WHAT MAKES THIS BOOK DIFFERENT?

Too many financial books and social media influencers try to sell a specific way to wealth, but this book is indifferent when it comes to how you get there. I've read many books where the author sells their special class, or their one way to wealth. The truth is, there are many ways to create wealth. Myself and our team of advisors work with millionaires every week who have worked hard and invested the dollars to achieve their goals. The reason the rich keep getting richer is because they think of their money differently than poor people do.

British historian Thomas Carlyle once said, "The best effect of any book is that it excites the reader to self-activity."[1] My goal is that through the story and basic visuals of understanding assets (green lights) vs. liabilities (red lights) is that you can grasp how to think differently about your finances and become a millionaire. I hope after reading this book you eliminate as many "red lights" as possible and hit as many "green lights" as possible to become a millionaire.

You may have heard the term "non-mortgage millionaire," which is someone who has a net worth of a million dollars outside of their home. As you will read in the upcoming chapters, the Green Light Millionaire is someone with assets (green lights) of a million dollars or more (not including their home equity), which help them grow their net worth each year.

As you read the stories of Joe Wealthy and Ben Broke, which opens each chapter, you can likely relate to both characters at various stages on their financial journeys. Think of Ben Broke as "been broke" in the past and Joe Wealthy as "you're wealthy" in the present. You can decide who you act like now, and who you want to act like moving forward.

We all have the ability through how we think and act to become wealthy or broke. Every day you make decisions that help you get closer to or farther away from becoming a millionaire. Your income has a smaller impact on your wealth than your ability to think differently about your finances. Each decision you make determines whether you will become wealthy or broke over your life. Think through which character you are most like now and which character you want to act like moving forward. After all, the way you think will impact your finances more than how much you make.

Let's go on this financial journey together.

🔒 WISDOM KEYS

Just like when you go to start a vehicle and need a key, there are various wisdom keys throughout the book. Use these wisdom keys to help you start thinking of your money in the appropriate way and use those keys to lay the foundation for guiding your financial journey.

CHAPTER 1

INTRODUCTION

Why the Way You Think Is How to Make Millions

Joe Wealthy and Ben Broke were best friends. They grew up in the same neighborhood, their parents worked similar jobs, and they came from normal "middle class" families. Neither had any major advantages or disadvantages financially speaking, but over the course of their lives they went different directions. Joe and Ben both started working in high school, went to college, and got decent paying jobs after school. While Joe ended up working a modest job at a factory, Ben was able to get into upper management and make at least 50 percent more than what Joe made throughout their working years.[1]

They got married the same year and ended up having kids the same age. They remained good friends throughout their working years and into the later years when they both wanted to retire at the same age. From the outside, it was almost like they had mirrored each other's lives.

---

[1] Hypothetical examples are for illustrative purposes only. Actual results will fluctuate with market conditions and will vary over time. There is no guarantee that similar results will be achieved.

But inside the households, it was a different story as Joe's net worth was significantly higher than Ben's. Joe's family had no debt, lived in a modest house, and drove used cars they bought with cash. Their family rarely ate out as they cooked meals at home and had dinner regularly as a family around the kitchen table. They didn't take out loans for anything. Since they had good cash flow, they were able to invest money every month toward their future goals.

In contrast, Ben's family lived in an upper-class neighborhood, and they had new luxury cars to park in their oversized garage. Ben's family also had a nice boat to take to the lake on the weekends. They all wore designer clothes to stay up to date on the latest styles. Ben's family made debt payments on their cars, home, boat, and other purchases each month. Ben's family typically ate out and rarely cooked meals at home. Even though Ben made good money, he invested very little each month toward his family's future goals.

When Joe and Ben were in their late fifties they were talking and were surprised to find out that Joe had a larger net worth than Ben and Joe could retire if he chose to. Since Ben had made significantly more money than Joe over the years, he was sure Joe had gotten lucky by winning a lottery or getting an inheritance from a random family member. The truth was Joe didn't play the lottery (he was too financially smart for that) and had yet to receive any kind of inheritance from anybody. Instead, Joe had been financially wise his entire life and made a lot of small financial decisions that snowballed into a large net worth in later years.

What made the difference between these two men over their lives? The way they thought about their finances was the key differentiator. Joe Wealthy understood the importance of assets that grew his wealth over time, while Ben Broke kept purchasing liabilities that made him more broke by the day. Joe became a millionaire and had the opportunity to retire early, while Ben had to keep working for many years to continue to pay for his house, cars, and other toys. Joe understood the importance of "green light" assets, while Ben kept sinking his money into "red light" liabilities. Through each chapter, we'll explore how each character and their thoughts about money changed the trajectory for their families for decades to come.

Imagine yourself on a journey to a place you have dreamed of going to for years. You have thought about this dream and talked about it. Now it's time to finally take the journey to achieve this dream. That end destination you want to reach may be different for you than anyone else, but we all have a destination in mind. So, you pack your vehicle and start on the journey, and you want to get there as fast as possible. Question: Do you want to hit a bunch of green lights on this journey or a bunch of red lights?

The answer seems obvious right? Of course, you want to hit a bunch of green lights as we all know green lights help us reach our destination faster than red lights. You have probably driven and hit a bunch of green lights in a row and were pleased as they made your journey smoother and ultimately you got to your destination faster than you had anticipated. This seems logical when it comes to driving across town for a meeting or appointment, but this same logic should also apply to achieving your financial goals.

When it comes to your financial goals, the reality is you are already in the vehicle and driving around. You likely already have an income of some kind and are working toward a future goal (retirement, generosity, home purchase, travel, etc.). Realistically many roads can get you to that end goal. You will have to cross through many intersections on your journey and potentially have to take detours as the route you wanted may no longer be available.

There are many avenues when it comes to creating wealth, and some are faster and slower than others. There are also choices on your financial journey that are not just slowing you down, but causing you to come to a complete stop and may hinder you from ever achieving your goals.

Red lights on your financial journey will slow you down and can potentially keep you from ever arriving at your destination. Only by hitting green lights consistently can you achieve your goals.

Consider this book a roadmap for your financial journey. No, this book won't give you the exact investment strategy (because there are many), nor will it give you the magic formula to become a millionaire (because there are multiple ways to achieve that status). The goal of this book is to get you to think differently. Every choice you make will either help or hurt your chances of reaching your end goal faster (or slower) depending on how you think about your finances.

I've known couples making $250,000/year with huge amounts of debt who can barely rub two nickels together, as well as couples making less than $100,000/year combined who are maxing out their retirement accounts and have a higher net worth. How is it possible for people to have such drastic income differences, but some achieve financial success with smaller incomes while others with larger incomes are barely getting by? The reason is because of differences in how people think about money.

How you think determines how you act, and how you act with your finances determines your potential to achieve your financial goals. Every dollar that comes to you allows you to invest in things that will either speed up your journey (assets or "green lights") or things that will slow down or stop your journey (liabilities or "red lights"). Thinking like the wealthy means putting your finances toward green lights that will help speed up your timeline to help achieve your goals.

Humans are visual learners. This is why we will use the visual analogy of traveling and coming across intersections and stop lights. Hopefully this visual aid will allow you to view your financial decisions differently. Every decision you make (especially early in your journey) impacts your timeline to your goal of wealth development. Moving forward, every dollar that leaves your pocket will either help you achieve your goals faster (green lights) or hinder your journey by slowing you down (red lights).

WHY NOT HAVE A SPECIFIC INVESTMENT PLAN IN THIS BOOK?

As a senior partner at a large wealth management practice and as a CERTIFIED FINANCIAL PLANNER™ (aka - CFP®), I understand that your financial plan is unique to you. Your goals, time horizons, risk tolerance, and income are all specific to you and your family. There is no cookie cutter approach when it comes to becoming a millionaire. I'm not writing this to sell you a certain investment or product, because there are many potential roads to get you to where you want to go. Instead, I am giving you a mindset that will work consistently on the road you choose for your life.

There are differences between principles and plans. Principles are things that are ongoing and don't change. That is the focus of this book. If you don't get principles right, the plan won't matter. Many different financial plans can help you, but you have to get the principles right to start. That's why you won't find a specific investment strategy, but you will find a strategy in how to think about your finances. Principles apply to every person reading this book.

Whether you are eighteen years old or eighty-eight years old, the principles in this book will apply to you. The specific plan that can be implemented may change, but the foundational principles need to be solid for long-term success. Principles are timeless and tireless. Principles don't wear out, rust out, or give out. Principles last forever. If you want to make rapid progress, don't fight against principles … flow with them. As Earl Riney once said, "Dollars do better when accompanied by sense."

The biggest influence in achieving your goals is not your investment account or your tax efficiencies. Your thinking is what can help you to achieve your goals faster or slower. Real estate, business ownership, 401k's, IRA's, brokerage accounts, and many other options are ways to help achieve financial success, but none of those will matter unless you can teach yourself to hit as many green lights as possible to help you become a millionaire.

One person's plan is another person's poison. This is why this book is not about a specific way to invest or create wealth. Other books and speakers may try to sell you on a specific investment (real estate, gold, crypto-currency, stocks, bonds, and annuities), but the sales pitches for those items are useless if you don't think like the wealthy think. What may work for one person may be disastrous for the next person. If you can think correctly about ways to help optimize each dollar, any one of those investments can assist in your journey.

Thoughts lead to feelings, which lead to actions, which lead to results. If you can change your thought process up front, it will help you achieve the results you want at the end. Personal financial success is 80 percent behavioral and only 20 percent head knowledge. You don't have to have a high IQ, a college degree, or be a valedictorian to build wealth. It's not about your intelligence; it's about your thoughts and choices. If you can get your thoughts right, you can get your actions right.

Terminology is key in your journey. How you define an "asset' or 'liability" can make or break your financial plan. There will likely be some ideas in this book that will challenge your current way of thinking and that is okay. Be willing to be teachable throughout your life and in a constant state of learning. That's another reason this book will not describe a certain way to invest. Investments can change over time, but how you think can help you continue to move forward no matter what assets you choose to invest in.

Budgeting won't be discussed at length in this book as there are other resources for that. The foundation for your financial journey is your ability to spend less than you earn, because every success in your financial life depends on this habit. If you can't spend less than you make, you can never succeed financially. This isn't an income issue; it's a financial maturity issue.

The quality of your life is determined by the quality of your thoughts. This is true in every area of your life, and that includes your finances. If others have what you want, examine their thoughts and how they think. Don't get mad at others for being successful; learn from them. Resenting the rich is one of the surest ways to stay broke. There are basic financial principles that can change the trajectory of your financial future and your family's future. Rich people focus on the rewards and opportunities, while the poor focus on the risks and obstacles.

The financially rich focus on making, keeping, growing, and even giving their money while the financially poor focus on spending their money. The difference between the rich and the poor is the rich invest their money and spend what's left, while the poor spend their money and invest what's left. Money flows from those who don't know how to manage it to those who know how to manage it. The reason the "rich keep getting richer" is because they follow solid financial principles every ... single ... day. Once you can grasp the basic concepts of this book you will also understand why wealthy families keep gaining wealth and why nothing is stopping you from also developing your wealth to pursue your financial goals.

In the chapters ahead we will look at various keys to think about your financial plan—things like why your personal home is NOT an asset and why a $7 coffee really hinders the journey (especially early on), as well as why all assets are not created equal, and why becoming a millionaire really isn't your goal. It is something deeper. Ultimately you don't want money, you want what money can do for you.

I've worked with hundreds of families to assist them in achieving their goals, and I hope this book helps you achieve your goals. Let's take this journey together and help you hit as many green lights as possible so you can achieve your goals as quickly as possible. As Albert Einstein once said, "Any fool can know. The point is to understand." Hopefully the following chapters help you understand these basic financial principles of success.

CHAPTER 2

GREEN LIGHTS

Assets: How Financial Wealth Is Developed

Joe Wealthy knew growing up that becoming a millionaire wasn't going to be easy. He was tempted his whole life to buy things on credit, but he mastered his temporary cravings. He stayed within his budget and every month invested funds toward his future goals. Joe realized early on that to be successful on his financial journey, he would need to hit as many green lights (assets) as he could that would help him develop his wealth long term. Every asset Joe added to his net worth worked on his behalf every year to grow his net worth until, eventually, he became a millionaire. Those assets were working even while Joe was sleeping or on vacation. While his friends drove new luxury vehicles and had bigger and better toys Joe was quietly investing money consistently into his investments which grew over time, creating more wealth for Joe and his family. Joe understood that the more assets and the larger the assets he could create, the more choices he would have in the future. Rather than feeding his desire for temporary pleasure, Joe chose to give his future self a gift, which grew exponentially over the years.[1]

---

[1] Investing involves the risk of loss that clients should be prepared to bear. No investment process is free of risk; no strategy or risk management technique can guarantee returns or eliminate risk in any market environment. There is no guarantee that your investment will be profitable. Past performance is not a guarantee of future performance.

Ben Broke barely saved any money on a consistent basis. He put funds aside in his 401k, but wasn't getting the full match because he had to ensure he could make the payments for all his liabilities. Since Ben was living on such a tight budget, he was nervous to put more funds aside. He needed the next paycheck to make the payments for his stuff. Ben had very little in assets due to his debt payments, and that only caused him to be more nervous as he got older and closer to retirement. Ben was so busy keeping up his lifestyle choices that his net worth barely grew each year. He couldn't gain momentum on building his assets that would help him grow his net worth. While Ben looked "rich" on the outside, the truth was he was one missed paycheck away from being severely hurt financially because he had very few real assets.

If you are going to consider assets to be the green lights on your journey and liabilities to be red lights, you need to understand the difference between the two. After all, if you don't know what an asset (green light) looks like you may be putting your money into things that are actually financial liabilities (red lights) that will hinder your ability to become financially successful.

Definitions are key! How would you define an asset? Your answer will have the biggest impact on how you create wealth for you and your family. Merriam-Webster's Dictionary describes an asset as "all the property of a person, corporation, or estate that may be used in payment of debts." According to Wikipedia an asset is, "any resource owned or controlled by a business or an economic entity." Is an asset really just something used to pay debts? Is a financial asset just a resource you control? The average person may use these resources to define an asset, but millionaires don't define an asset this way.

ASSET:

Something that puts money into your pocket

This is the definition I invite you to use moving forward in your financial journey. Too many times, people list liabilities as assets. Don't confuse a net worth statement with an asset. Sure, your vehicle may have value but it is NOT a financial asset. Even if you have a vehicle paid for, it will cost you money every month (gas, insurance, license fees, and repairs).

An asset may not put money in your pocket immediately, but it should continue to grow in value and put money back into your pocket on a constant basis, which allows you to buy more assets and grow your net worth over time. Examples can include things like 401k's, IRA's, real estate, bonds, mutual funds, CD's, owning a business, etc. In-depth examples will be given in chapter five.

How about your personal residence? Is it an asset? Based on our definition of an asset as something that puts money into your pocket, your personal residence is not an asset (even though it may be listed on a net worth statement). I'm not saying you shouldn't own a home, and an entire chapter will be dedicated to home ownership. I just need you to understand why your home should never be considered a financial asset. The wealthy understand that their personal residence is not a tool to build wealth long term.

Again, an asset is something that puts money in your pocket. Even if you pay off your mortgage and are "debt free," your home still costs you money every month with taxes, insurance, utilities, repairs, and updating. More on this in an upcoming chapter, but since a home is likely the largest financial purchase a family will make, it needs to be addressed up front.

If you want to build wealth and put money in your pocket, the key will be to put your money into assets as early and often as you possibly can. The earlier you can put money into assets and as often as possible, the better you will be long term. The problem for most people is they put money into things that are not assets and wonder why they get to their forties and have little or no net worth built up.

If you are constantly buying items that are not putting money in your pocket, you can never expect to become a millionaire. Rich people have their money work hard for them. Poor people work hard for their money. Every dollar that comes your way is an opportunity to build wealth or an obstacle that can hinder your ability to become a millionaire.

My wife used to play this game when we were first married where she would ask me what I would do with the money if we ever won the lottery. This was a game because I refused to waste money on a lottery or gambling. Every time she asked me this question I gave her the exact same answer. I would invest the entire amount to build our net worth and create more cash flow for our family. My wife would get frustrated and say my answer was "boring" because she wanted me to say things like house upgrades, cars, and vacations. It's not that those things are wrong, but I know that investing in assets is what makes millionaires different from those who struggle financially. Eventually my wife tried to get her answer by asking, "After you invested your lottery winnings, what would you use the cashflow to buy?" I would laugh and jokingly tell her "more assets" ... to which she would roll her eyes and then tell me how she would spend "our cash flow."

🔒 WISDOM KEY:

Let your assets pay for your liabilities.

I'm not saying that updating a house, buying a newer vehicle, or going on vacations is bad. My wife and I have done these things and will continue to do these things. Your home is a place to raise a family and create memories, and vacations are great ways to create moments to remember for the rest of your life. Just understand that your assets can pay for those things for you long term. Your assets can pay for your vacations, vehicles, and home updates; then you don't have to use your income for that. Too many people put their money into their personal home, vehicle, and other financial liabilities that hinder their ability to create wealth in the long run.

This key knowledge is exactly why the "rich keep getting richer." It's not that the wealthy are stealing from the poor. It's that wealthy individuals and families understand that wealth is developed over time through growing assets. This is why giving money to people who don't understand the differences between assets and liabilities will never work. Unless you can understand the importance of putting your money into assets, you will not become wealthy or pass any real wealth to the next generation. Don't believe me? Just research the people who have won millions of dollars in the lottery and were financially broke again in less than five to seven years. They spent all their money on liabilities and never changed their income or net worth long term.

🔒 WISDOM KEY:

All assets should be connected with a specific goal.

Once you start to put money into assets, be sure each of those assets is connected with a specific goal. We will talk more about goals in a later chapter, but your goals are what drive your financial plan and determine where your assets should be invested. This is exactly why this book is not about a specific plan, rather about principles to help you become wealthy and achieve your goals.

Keep in mind that not all assets are created equal. Money

in short-term vehicles (checking or savings accounts, CD, money market, bonds, etc.) can be great for your short-term goals, but likely aren't the best options for long-term goals like retirement. On the flip side for short-term goals, you don't want to invest in things that can be volatile or difficult to access. Things like stocks, growth mutual funds, businesses, and real estate can have dangers in the short term with volatile ups and downs of the stock market or liquidity issues with real estate or a business. It's not that any of these investment vehicles are right or wrong. You just need to ensure that every asset is attached to a specific goal and a time horizon to be appropriately invested for your future.

Business ownership is one of the best ways to create wealth. There are definitely risks involved with any business startup, but the rewards can be amazing for those willing to take a calculated risk. Business ownership allows you to be in control of your future because you don't have an employer telling you what to do. Investing in yourself and your business can be some of the greatest investments you make, but just keep in mind you need to have an "exit plan." I've worked with business owners who were ready to retire and had trouble selling their businesses because it was a self-employed situation where the new owner would have to work a lot of hours.

Again, any asset you have should be attached to a goal of some kind and that includes business ownership. Always keep the end in mind on what you want your life to look like in the future and get assets in place to help you achieve those goals. The key is to understand that in order to continue growing your wealth, you have to put money toward assets that will help you achieve your goals.

When you are investing in assets, you want to keep in mind that tax efficiencies can have a BIG impact on your net worth long term. Make sure your assets are as tax efficient as they can be. Utilizing vehicles like 401k's and IRA's can be great ways to help you make sure your net worth isn't taking big tax hits.

Those who invest in their own business or real estate can also take advantage of the tax breaks that can come with those assets. Make sure you have a team of people who can assist with your tax efficiencies. Be sure to educate yourself on whether Roth vs. Traditional retirement accounts are best for you and consult someone who can assist with this journey. It's much more cost-effective to learn from others and the mistakes they have seen instead of making the mistakes yourself.

🔒 WISDOM KEY:
Things that last typically aren't built fast.

When it comes to creating wealth, you need to understand this is likely a long-term play for you. Yes, people hit it big with a lottery win or a specific company that grows like crazy … but those are the exceptions. And, as we said earlier, even winning the lottery often does not translate directly into wealth. Be cautious of trying to time the market or put funds into a specific company your buddy told you is supposed to do well. I've worked with multiple clients to help build sound financial plans that are well diversified and tax efficient. Many people say they want "financial security." Just remember this acronym for Financial SECURITY: Security Earned Carefully Usually Results In Treasure-filled Years.

I have no problems if people want to invest in single companies or a single market sector they think will do well this next quarter, but if you aren't maximizing IRA accounts and employer plans, I would encourage you to keep building a stronger foundation financially before trying to hit it big. The concern is that when people are trying to buy a single stock for a quick buck it's similar to gambling or speculation. Keep your focus on building a solid foundation before getting too quickly into specific areas that could hinder your long-term goals.

To business owners specifically, I caution against putting everything in one basket (your business). Yes, as a business owner myself I have taken risks that were all calculated. Just like I would caution anyone against investing in just a single stock, I would also caution against having no other investments outside of a company. Make sure you are still putting funds aside that can be diversifying your assets to ensure your entire financial plan isn't relying on a single entity. You can set up a retirement plan through your business to diversify long-term assets to help with this.[2]

Many people like to keep things as simple as possible when it comes to finances which can allow you to hit some green lights automatically without having to think about it. Having systematic contributions into your investment accounts can be a great way to achieve green lights without extra effort. Whether it's through your employer's 401k or your own IRA account, you can set this up and not have to think about it each month.

This can be tougher with other assets like real estate or businesses where cash flow can change monthly, but having systems for your finances is like putting your financial plan on cruise control. It allows you to relax more and enjoy the journey without having so much stress from each transaction. Examples of this could include automatic contributions in your 401(k) from your paycheck or monthly contributions into a Roth IRA from your bank account. Maybe your next step is to put a SYSTEM in place for your finances. SYSTEM—Save Your Self Time, Energy, and Money.

---

[2] Diversification does not guarantee a profit or protect against loss in a declining market. They are methods used to help manage investment risk.

CHAPTER 3

RED LIGHTS

Liabilities: How Financial Wealth Is Destroyed

Joe Wealthy avoided liabilities at all costs. He understood the liabilities made him go backwards every month instead of helping him achieve his goal of becoming a millionaire. After school, Joe never took out any debt (besides his mortgage), and his school loans were paid off in less than two years. By the time he paid off his fifteen-year mortgage, he had no liabilities left and was only in his mid-forties. Joe's family saved cash for any purchases which included vacations or house updates. Since they had no liabilities, their cash flow each month left them with excess to put toward their future goals. Even though they could afford excessive living, Joe and his family continued to live within a budget and invested 15 percent (or more) each month as well as gave more than 10 percent each month to their church and other causes that were important to them.

Ben Broke collected liabilities like some kids collect sports cards. After paying the mortgage, car loans, boat loan, credit cards, and other lines of credit (for things like furniture), Ben had barely anything left to put toward his goals. Any extra seemed to go toward trying to pay off their most recent vacation. This didn't include all the money the Broke family spent on eating out and entertainment each month. Not only was their family barely keeping up, they were slowly falling more and more behind each month. Ben would love to give more to his church and other charities, but at this point, he had no extra funds due to the amount of excess spending. All the "red light" liabilities they keep hitting every month destroyed their ability to create wealth and become millionaires long term.

Anytime you take a journey, you want to reach your final destination as quickly and smoothly as possible. If you go on vacation or meet up with friends for a night out, you don't look for the route that takes the longest. If you use any kind of map software to travel, you know the software will give you multiple options at times, but the fastest route is typically the one chosen. If you were with a friend to join up with others for dinner, you would get frustrated if they intentionally went slow and tried to hit as many red lights as possible. We all understand that a red light is something that can slow (or completely stop) your progress.

While this is an easy concept to understand when it comes to traveling, most people hit "red lights" all the time when it comes to their finances. Sometimes this is done intentionally, and sometimes by accident, but every time you hit a red light with your finances, it hurts your chance of building wealth and becoming a millionaire in the long run. Red lights come in many forms, and the key is to understand what a red light is so you can plan your financial journey accordingly to allow you to avoid them as much as possible.

RED LIGHT (LIABILITY)

Anything that takes away from assets and hinders your long-term wealth development.

A financial "red light" will do one of two things. It can either slow you down from achieving your goals by causing you to hit fewer financial green lights, or potentially put you in a place where you will never accomplish your financial goals.

Red lights financially come in many forms, and like green lights (assets), not all red lights are created equal. Just like when you are driving, you may hit a red light but slow down just a little before it turns green; or sometimes it feels like you are at a standstill for hours and will never move. Certain financial red lights can just slow you down a little, and others will cause you to make a complete stop for weeks or months depending on how bad the red-light decision is. You can't address all red-light items immediately, but there should be areas that need to be addressed first before trying to work on other red-light items in your finances.

🔒 WISDOM KEY:

It's not how much you make, it's how much you keep.

Debts are the biggest and longest red lights on your financial journey. Any non-mortgage debt should be taken care of as soon as possible. Mortgages will be addressed in the next chapter, but this chapter will focus on any debts outside of the mortgage. When you think of debt I'm also referring to personal debt and not business debt. While I believe any debt should be avoided, if possible, there are certain businesses that are hard to make successful without some type of business loan.

We have many clients who are business owners or farmers, and they can use debt wisely with their business to help them build an asset (their business) which then generates money toward wealth development. Good luck trying to come up with a seven-figure payment for farm equipment. I'm not saying you should intentionally try and get as many business loans as possible, but for this section I'm going to reference personal debt and why everything non-mortgage should get paid off ASAP.

🔒 **WISDOM KEY:**

You can't get to your long-term goals with your parking brake on.

Debts are the items on your financial journey that work against you every single month. You are going to be at a standstill at that red light, and your journey toward creating wealth is going to be hindered as long as you are paying off debts. Whether it's credit cards, vehicles, school loans, personal loans, or medical bills, you want these items eliminated as quickly as possible. I've never met a millionaire who credits their car or furniture payments in helping them create wealth. Think about putting on your parking brake as you sit at the red light ... that is what debt does to you financially. Depending on how severe your debt is it may even be like putting the car in reverse and going backwards for a time period.

Another term I use to get the point across is the "Stupid Tax." The Stupid Tax is any fee or interest paid on items that takes money away from your assets. It doesn't matter if it's furniture, vehicles, clothing, or entertainment. If you are paying fees and interest on these items, you are getting destroyed by the Stupid Tax. Buying things for immediate gratification is a futile attempt to make up for dissatisfaction in life, and this practice reveals a lack of discipline and maturity in your thinking.

If you don't have the money to purchase the item, you shouldn't be buying it ... no excuses. If you have non-mortgage debt, it's time to take your goals seriously and get that debt paid off as soon as possible. Stop sitting at the red lights of your financial journey waiting for someone else to do something. Ignorance is not bliss. Ignorance is poverty. Your financial goals are much more valuable than anything on credit that makes you feel good at the moment.

There are basically two main ways to think about paying off your debts. You need to know yourself and how you are wired to choose which option is best for you. This is more mental than financial. Figure out how you are motivated and sprint to get rid of all non-mortgage debt as soon as possible. Both of these options are typically referred to as a "snowball" method of debt reduction.

1. Debts from smallest amount to largest amount: List all your debts from smallest to largest amounts. Do not worry about interest rates right now. Start paying off debts beginning with the smallest amount and work your way through each debt until they are all eliminated. I typically find this is the most motivating way to work through the debt snowball as you get some short-term wins to keep you motivated to keep paying off those debts.

2. Debts from highest interest rate to lowest interest rate: This method is similar in thought but lists all debts in order of interest rates from highest to lowest (debt amount doesn't matter). If you can truly stay focused, this is the most effective way to pay down debt as you eliminate the higher interest rates first.

With either method the goal is to get any non-mortgage debt eliminated as quickly as possible. Be honest with yourself and how you view money. If you are still paying off debt, the best scenario is likely the debt snowball with the smallest amounts first, but figure out what keeps you motivated. We will talk about motivation and goals in a later section of this book.

Your financial goals will be the key to staying locked in and focused on paying loans down. I've encouraged clients to have pictures of certain goals to keep them focused on what they want long term. Others have used a visual like a thermometer that slowly fills in as the final debts are paid. I don't care what method you choose, but choose the method that motivates you the most.

Once all your non-mortgage debts are paid down, the journey toward wealth development is just beginning. Too many people have their big goal of "being debt free" which is a nice thought and I think you should avoid debt as much as possible, but isn't life more than just being debt free? I hope you see your financial journey and end goals as not just avoiding credit card and car payments, but as something much bigger that excites you long term. That's why the goals chapter of this book is key to help keep you motivated past just paying off debt.

Other red lights are items that will continue to slow you down on your journey toward wealth development. While we could talk about a lot of areas, I will focus on a couple of key areas I often see that hinder people from becoming wealthy and ultimately hinder them in achieving their goals even after the non-mortgage debt is paid off.

People typically part with their money for two main reasons: to solve a problem and to attain good feelings. Think about your personal finances and the money you spend on things that are not assets. Some of the purchases solve a problem (housing or transportation), but many miscellaneous purchases are just to attain a good feeling.

Eating out and entertainment are likely the biggest areas I often see people hitting the brakes on their financial journey. I'm always amazed at how much people spend on eating out and food delivery services. This can be a complete waste of money and hinder your wealth development over time. I'm not saying you should never eat out. I actually encourage clients who hit a financial goal (like paying off a major loan or being debt free) to celebrate with a meal with family or friends. I understand it's easy to pull through the drive-through or open up the app and have someone deliver food, but this is a red-light item every time.

Maybe this visual of red lights and green lights will help

keep you motivated as you drive home from work. Have a visual of your financial goals, and when you are tempted to swing through the drive-through or order something to go, be reminded that it is a red light that will hinder your wealth development.

I work with clients constantly who are millionaires, and I've never had a client list "eating out" as one of their financial goals. Those who understand wealth know they need to put their money toward green lights and avoid red light items as much as possible on their financial journey.

Vehicles are also common red-light decisions. Your vehicle is NOT an asset and costs money every single month which takes money away from your true assets (green lights) that help create wealth. Every month your vehicle gets a little more mileage or a little more wear and tear. I understand that newer vehicles are necessary at times (especially for growing families), but you don't need all the special features that cost more money.

Ultimately you want your vehicle to get you from one place to another. Don't try to impress others with what you drive. Many people who drive nicer vehicles are either leasing those vehicles or have high monthly payments. I don't care if your interest rate is 0.9 percent on the vehicle. Your vehicle costs you money every month and will not help you develop wealth. The best vehicle for you to drive … the one that is paid off.

There are many other items we could discuss in this chapter, but I wanted to give you a way to think about your debts and finances. Again, this book is not about a specific route to take. This is about thinking of your finances differently so you can strive to become a millionaire and achieve your financial goals in the future. Yes, I think you should have a budget that guides all dollars that come in and out. If you begin with a wrong pattern of thinking, a budget will eventually flop. You need to think correctly about your money in order to win financially.

Financial maturity is key when it comes to managing your finances. Financial maturity is being able to give up today's desires for future benefits. Why don't we allow seven-year-olds to drive vehicles on the road? The child is not mature enough to handle a big vehicle. We allow young adults to get a license once they can prove themselves trustworthy by passing a test, but when it comes to finances there is no official test to pass. You just get the keys to your financial vehicle whether you are ready to drive or not. Be honest with yourself about your financial maturity and if you need extra guidance in this area. There are a lot of grown adults acting like seven-year-old children sitting behind the wheel of their financial vehicle.

🔒 **WISDOM KEY:**

Have an account just for "fun" for you and your family.

The last item I will address is putting aside dollars for "fun" each month for you and your family. This is probably the most boring chapter in the book. I get it ... paying off debt and talking about budgeting is not fun, but if you can't get that right foundationally, you are in trouble. My wife and I each give ourselves "blow money" each month. These funds are to be used in any way we want, and we can "blow" the money on any items we choose without worrying about those dollars impacting our long-term goals.

Make sure this amount is small at the beginning as you will want to build assets that can fund your goals and spending in the future. Let your assets pay for your fun so your paycheck doesn't have to. Once your assets are paying for your fun you are starting to think like the truly wealthy who use assets to pay for their lifestyle.

CHAPTER 4

YELLOW LIGHTS

Personal Home: Why It Is Not an Asset

Joe Wealthy knew that owning a home was import-
ant for his family. While paying rent, he knew the landlord would be the one building equity long term and also
get the appreciation on the property in years to come. Joe
also understood that his personal residence would not be an
asset for him financially as it would always cost him money
(even when it was paid off). Joe saved up a good downpayment of 20 percent on his home and put the mortgage on
a fifteen-year loan to ensure he didn't have payments for
decades into the future. The house the Wealthy family purchased was within their means, and without any other debts
they still had good monthly cash flow even with a mortgage
payment. Instead of putting more money into his personal
residence, Joe Wealthy chose to live modestly and grow his
assets which allowed him financial freedom in his fifties and
have the choice to retire and give generously as he desired.

Ben Broke took a different route when it came to his
home purchase. Due to his many liabilities, he wasn't able
to save up 20 percent for a downpayment and had to pay
PMI (Private Mortgage Insurance) which only increased

his monthly payments. The Broke family also had to put the home on a thirty-year mortgage as they couldn't afford the payments of a fifteen-year mortgage, which would mean they could still be making mortgage payments when they were hoping to retire. Ben was told his house was an "asset" as it would appreciate in value over time, but the problem for Ben was that with the mortgage payments, taxes, insurance, utilities, and general upkeep, the house cost him money every month. Instead of waiting to have 20 percent down, Ben overextended himself with his house, and his personal home turned into a financial burden instead of a family blessing.

Okay, I can already see the emails coming into my inbox or posts from mortgage bankers and realtors telling me how a home is an asset because it builds equity over time and how historically, home values increase over time. Yes, I agree that homes will increase in value over time and that you can build equity in the long run. Yes, I do believe you should own your own home rather than rent so as property values rise you can gain that long-term equity. My goal in this chapter (like the goal for this entire book) is to get you to think differently when it comes to your personal residence and how that home can help or hinder your ability to create long-term wealth for you and your family.

Think of the yellow lights you come across any time you travel. You approach an intersection and the light is blinking yellow. This doesn't mean you have to come to a complete stop, but you are put on notice to be careful when approaching this intersection because it's not a green light giving you permission to go right through. You go a little slower with yellow lights than green, and even though you typically don't stop completely, the yellow lights don't help you travel any faster.

Yellow lights are a sign that you should proceed with caution. That is exactly why your home purchase needs a yellow light. This is likely the biggest purchase you will ever make, and you need to think this through. The decisions that go into a home purchase will likely have a six-figure impact on your wealth development.

You want your home to be a blessing to you and not a burden financially. The focus of your home should be about making memories with friends and family for portraits, not about trying to make payments. Making memories is way more fun than being concerned about making payments. So, if the home you bought grows in value over time and builds equity along the way, which increases your net worth, why is your home a yellow light?

🔒 **WISDOM KEY:**

Your home is not a financial asset.

I feel the need to say this multiple times to reinforce this idea because it is likely new to you. As I've mentioned multiple times, definitions are key to your financial success, and they determine how you think about everything you have. Remember, an asset is something that puts money IN your pocket. Your personal residence will NEVER do this. Your personal home will always take money OUT of your pocket every single month as long as you own it.

This is also why I don't typically recommend clients put a bunch of extra money toward their mortgage. Even when the home is paid off, it will still cost you money every month through insurance, taxes, utilities, maintenance, and improvements. Yes, your payments will decrease without principal and interest, but your home will still cost you money every month as long as you live there.

The exact strategy of paying off your home may depend on interest rates and your goals. I've had clients with very low interest rates (less than 3%), who paid large amounts toward the mortgage each month. I would tell them that

I can't come up with a good stewardship argument to do that vs. invest the dollars long term, but paying off their mortgage was their top financial goal and that is what they wanted. Paying off the mortgage is a positive step and will create more cash flow, but in comparison to green lights, this is still a yellow light way of thinking about wealth development.

For most people their home is a very personal decision which also causes it to be an emotional decision. The emotional part of the decision isn't bad. In fact, it's a good thing because your home is the place where you raise a family, spend time with friends, and create memories to be cherished for a lifetime. These emotions are also the reason your home is a yellow light when it comes to wealth development.

It can be easy to go over budget on a home purchase as monthly payments aren't impacted too much, but that added debt payment over time only hinders your ability to become financially free. Constantly updating your house with new flooring, wall colors, and decorations takes money OUT of your pocket every time.

Anytime you go through an intersection with blinking yellow lights you are more cautious as you have to watch for other cars and pedestrians who are using that intersection. This forces you to be more patient in your journey and the same is true for your home purchase. Be patient and take time to figure out an exact budget for your home.

Key tips for your current and future home purchases.

- Put 20 percent down to avoid having to pay PMI (Private Mortgage Insurance).
- Work to get a fifteen-year fixed rate mortgage. This allows you to pay off the home quicker to create long-term cash flow and also helps lock in the principal/interest amount so you know what to expect in future years.
- Keep the mortgage payment to 25 percent of your net monthly income.

- Before paying any extra on your mortgage payment, have a clear picture of your goals and which goals have the highest priority. If being 100 percent debt free is your top goal, then consider putting some extra toward that; but if the mortgage payment is 25 percent of net income or less and it doesn't stress your finances, consider putting extra toward your retirement or other future goals that are in wealth-building (green light) assets.

My wife and I have purchased a home that was in fore-closure from a bank. We ended up getting a great deal on the home financially as the bank wanted to sell it quickly, and we had been patient in our home-buying process. If banks are all about making money, why do they get rid of them so quickly when the homeowner can't make their payments? Banks understand that the home isn't the asset; the debt on the home is the asset which makes the banks money.

Just be mindful of your home in regard to how you see it financially. Your home is a great tool for hosting friends and family and creating some fantastic memories, but it's not a good tool for building assets and creating wealth for yourself long term. Let your home be a blessing to you and not a burden financially. Focus on the green lights and be cautious of the yellow light of your personal residence.

A strategy that can work if you are willing to make sac-rifices is "house hacking." This can allow your personal residence to help create cashflow. Basically with "house hacking" you either rent out a certain room (or rooms) of your home or you purchase some kind of multi-family prop-erty like a duplex where you live on one side and rent out the other half. This is another great way to help reduce living expenses to allow better cash flow each month for you to continue to build assets.

My wife and I also did this early on when we had a duplex we lived in. It was a fantastic way to keep expenses as low as possible and invest in assets early in life, which gave us freedom in lifestyle choices later when we had children. This option is not for everyone as many don't want to be a landlord or share a wall with another family, but "house hacking" executed properly can definitely speed up your ability to create wealth long term.

CHAPTER 5

ASSETS

Not All Assets Are Created Equal

Since Joe Wealthy had set a solid foundation financially, he was able to put every extra dollar toward his long-term goals. Joe's family had a fully funded emergency reserve, and with no debts outside of their mortgage, they could put all extra funds toward their specific goals. Joe invested 15 percent (sometimes more) into long-term accounts which include his 401k and Roth IRA, and they also invested in a separate account outside of retirement accounts that they can utilize in future years prior to retirement. Since they have all the short- and mid-term needs met, the Wealthy family can put all the focus on their long-term goals to ensure every dollar is invested appropriately for the long term.

Ben Broke was in a very different financial position with his assets. He barely had enough to get the full match from his employer. Since the Broke family did not have a fully funded emergency reserve, he had to try and put extra funds toward this each month. The biggest problem was tight cash flow, which caused them to dip into this fund constantly to cover extra expenses. Since their bank accounts paid little interest, they could not gain traction on their long-term assets. The extra percent they gained in a high yield savings didn't make the impact needed for the long run. Ben's long-term retirement goals couldn't be accomplished while he had to put any extra funds toward short-term accounts just to take care of short- and mid-term needs. The quicker Ben could reduce debt payments and increase cash flow, the quicker he could put more money toward his long-term assets to build up wealth for him and his family.

Just like when you pull up a destination on GPS or any kind of mapping software, you typically get multiple routes. Similarly, there is no one set way to create wealth for you and your family.

The key moving forward is to understand how every green light is not created equal. Even though you are investing in assets, you want to ensure each of them is tied to a specific goal. Most people typically have short- (1-3 year), mid- (4-6 year) and long- (7+ year) term goals when it comes to their finances, and you want to make sure every dollar is in the appropriate asset to ensure you strategically use it.

🔒 **WISDOM KEY:**

Assets should travel at the speed of your goals.

Here are visuals of different assets and how fast they can travel.

- Short-term assets = School Zones
- Mid-term assets = Residential or Commercial Streets
- Long-term assets = Interstates and Highways

Even though each asset helps you move forward, it may be helpful to think of them in regard to the speed in which you can travel. The shorter time horizon on the goal should equate to smaller returns of money. The longer time horizon on the goal, the higher returns should be. You don't want fast-moving assets in short-term goals that can cause major setbacks and damage you and your family financially. The opposite is true for your long-term goals. You want higher returns for funds that are more aggressive so you can travel as fast as possible to achieve wealth development in the long run.

Think of your short-term goals like driving through a school zone. You go at a slow pace because there are always potential obstacles. It's good to go slow in these areas to protect yourself and those around you. Your mid-term goals are like traveling through areas that have commercial and residential properties. You can go faster than a school zone but you still have to be mindful of other vehicles and pedestrians. You can afford to be more aggressive with your speed, but you still can't go as fast as the interstate.

For your long-term goals, you can afford to be more aggressive (or risky) as you have long-term time horizons to adjust with potential setbacks in the market or your business. Just like on the interstate, you can travel much faster than in a school zone. Your long-term goals should be invested in assets that over the long run produce higher rates of return than your short-term goals. Why pursue your goals at 15mph when you can travel at 65?

Short-term assets for short-term goals—Examples: checking, savings, money market, CD's, and mutual funds that are all or highly bond based.

These accounts are assets as you typically get some type of interest, but it's usually minimal. Of your short-, mid-, and long-term assets, this bucket should typically be your smallest amount. The only exception is if you are preparing for a major purchase in the short term like a vehicle, down-payment on a house, or other major expense. Otherwise just keep enough in these accounts to pay the bills and have at least $1,000 extra for any quick emergency expenses that may arise. You don't want to keep putting money on credit or loans for random short-term expenses, so have a little extra to protect yourself in the short term.

NOTE—Don't waste a bunch of time trying to find the best interest rate for short-term accounts. You should keep minimal amounts in these accounts, and your mental focus is better spent on long-term wealth creation. No one ever becomes a millionaire by getting an extra 0.5 percent on their emergency fund in a savings account. You need to keep your mental focus on the big picture of wealth development. Yes, be a wise steward and try to earn as much as possible, but becoming wealthy won't happen in these types of accounts. Your time is better invested in focusing on long-term goals. Don't spend a dollar's worth of time on a ten-cent decision.

Mid-term assets for mid-term goals—Examples: bonds (higher yield), long-term CD's, and mutual funds that have a mixture of stocks/bonds.

These accounts are typically referred to as "moderate" accounts or investments because they don't have short time horizons. You want to get some growth on the money, but you aren't trying to hit a grand slam and get massive rates of return. The reason for that is massive returns can also come with massive losses, and if you have an upcoming purchase, that may be hindered by a big drop in the market.

You want decent liquidity tied to these goals as you don't have a long time horizon. You likely want to avoid any investment that will have liquidity issues or surrender charges. Most clients we work with like a diversified investment of stocks/bonds to strategically invest dollars for their risk tolerance but still have liquidity so they can access the funds if needed.

NOTE—Since these accounts will likely have higher balances than the short-term accounts, you want to ensure these are appropriately invested. Take the time to know your time horizon for these goals and invest the dollars appropriately. If a home purchase is four to five years away, you want those funds growing as much as possible without taking on too much risk. Again, take the time to make sure these dollars are invested appropriately, but these accounts are not designed for wealth development long term.

Your long-term wealth development comes from long-term goals and investments. You may not have any funds in this bucket, depending on your goals. If short-term items are taken care of and all your other goals are long term, just focus on growing the money as much as possible for your future.

Long-term assets for long-term goals—Examples: growth mutual funds or ETF's, single stocks, real estate, and business ownership.

This is where the largest majority of your money should be. Even as we work with our retired, or soon-to-be retired clients, we typically keep a large majority of their funds in a growth bucket. This obviously varies for each individual/family depending on the risk tolerance and time horizon, but if you are not going to use the funds for 7+ years, you will want to keep these dollars growing as much as possible.

One of the biggest mistakes I have seen clients make is going too conservative too quickly with a majority of their funds. This is why having every dollar attached to a goal is so vital. It helps you steward and invest every dollar wisely to ensure your goal of wealth development can be achieved. For many people these types of assets are for retirement, but we also have clients we invest aggressively for long-term wealth accumulation goals.

🔒 WISDOM KEY:
Taxes are Uncle Sam's friend, not yours.

A major part of wealth development is being as tax efficient as possible on your financial journey. You don't want to have a major tax drag on your wealth as that only hinders your finances. You don't put a large parachute on the back of your vehicle when you travel, so think of taxes as a parachute you want to keep as small as possible on your financial vehicle. We work with clients every day on their tax efficiency with their financial plans.

The more money you keep in your pocket, the more you have to invest moving forward. Wealth is created when money and assets are in your name, not the federal government's. Make sure you are working with someone who is helping you be as tax efficient as possible in developing your long-term wealth development.

Examples of tax efficient vehicles can include items like 401k, 403b, IRA, and Roth accounts (these are commonly referred to as "retirement accounts") for tax efficiency on your investments. Business owners can take advantage of many tax deductions depending on the type of business. Real estate can provide depreciation and tax deferral benefits as well.

There are three main categories that your money is taxed: Tax Now, Tax Later, and Tax Never.

- **Tax Now** = CD, brokerage account, checking/savings, and dividends.
- **Tax Later** = 401k, 403b, IRA, and sale of appreciated assets.
- **Tax Never** = Roth (IRA and 401k), HSA, and municipal bonds (at a federal level).[1]

There are pros/cons to each of the categories depending on your goals. Just make sure that tax efficiency is a part of your overall financial strategy to achieve your goals faster.

Many people follow a three-step progression to being tax efficient in their retirement accounts. This three-step progression helps you be as tax efficient as possible with your long-term retirement dollars.

---

[1] Roth and HSA withdrawals are income tax free as long as certain qualifying conditions are met.

1. First, get the maximum match from your employer plan (if applicable).
2. Second, contribute the maximum amount annually to your own Roth IRA or Traditional IRA.
3. Third, go back to your employer plan and increase contributions until you are investing 15 percent (or more) into your retirement accounts.

If your health insurance plan is HSA-eligible, a Health Savings Account can be an excellent tool for tax efficiency. HSAs offer triple tax benefits: tax-deductible contributions, tax-deferred growth, and tax-free withdrawals for qualified medical expenses. There are specific eligibility requirements, but it's worth checking if you qualify so you can take advantage of this type of account.

You should be cautious with any asset tied to insurance, such as annuities or permanent life insurance. While these can technically be considered assets since they may grow over time, they often come with higher fees and charges compared to straightforward investment options. Just like you want to avoid tax drag on your investments, you also want to avoid the "insurance drag" that can reduce your overall returns.

That's not to say these tools don't have a place, but in most cases, it makes more sense to focus on assets primarily designed to grow your net worth rather than those that try to both grow and protect it.

My goal as I work with clients is to grow their assets as quickly as possible to help them self-insure as quickly as possible. Instead of having to pay out extra money for insurance each month, you can just grow your net worth. Again, I'm trying to get you to think in a growth mindset rather than a scarcity mindset. Almost every time you run a scenario comparing term insurance and investing the difference in long-term investments vs. paying for permanent life insurance, the term life insurance wins in the long run. If you want to become a multi-millionaire, you have to focus on assets that can help your wealth grow as quickly and efficiently as possible.

Some assets have a "storage of value." These could be items like gold, cryptocurrency, precious metals, etc. I've even had clients use sports cards or collectible cars as storage of value. Just keep in mind that items like these don't put money in your pocket like other assets we have discussed. Your hope with these items is that someone else later on will pay you more for the item than what you paid for it. They likely are not paying you any interest or dividend along the way and can potentially have liquidity issues. While items that store value can have a place in a financial plan, long term you will likely want the bulk of your assets in a place that can grow in value as well as pay you along the way.

CHAPTER 6

GOALS

The Real Reason You Do (or Don't) Accumulate Wealth

Joe Wealthy and his family had clear financial goals. Having a crystal-clear picture of their goals allowed them to stay focused each month on where their dollars went. When they were tempted to eat out each week, they realized those meals were red light items that would hinder their wealth development. They would rather have financial freedom long term and put extra funds toward those goals each month and continually grow their net worth. Because of the compounding rate of return on green light assets, eventually the Wealthy family had more money coming in from their assets each month than what they made from their jobs! This gave them total financial freedom to do the things they wanted. Staying focused on their goals every day was the catalyst that helped them properly steward every dollar that came through their plan.

Ben Broke and his family also had financial goals. They wanted to retire by age sixty, travel, have a 2nd home down south, give to their church and other causes important to them, and leave a legacy for their kids. Unfortunately for the Broke family, their spending didn't align with their goals. They ate out multiple nights a week and went into debt for home upgrades and new vehicles. They spent more money on eating out than they did their kids' college, and they spent more money on their car payments each month than they invested in their retirement accounts. At some point the Broke family will have to look reality in the mirror and understand that their goals are not really their goals until they start funding them appropriately. The Broke family could tell you what their goals were, but their real goals and desires were displayed through their spending habits. Their healthy long-term goals were merely dreams and fantasies until they could begin putting money into green light assets that could make their dreams come true.

Whenever you travel with others, you know what your end goal is before you even start planning for the journey. This is common sense when it comes to traveling on a vacation. If you are in Chicago and want to go to Disneyland in California, you know that heading East will take you in the opposite direction. You instantly know that path would not line up with your ultimate goal.

The problem for most people is they don't actually know what they want. As I work with clients we talk extensively through goals. It's not uncommon when I first bring up the topic of their goals to get blank stares or shoulder shrugs as they have never thought of what they actually want their lives to look like. Forget about willpower; it's time to build your "why-power."

Take a moment to think about and write down where you want to go on your financial journey. What do you want your life to look like? Try and be as specific as possible with your goals. The most common term I hear people say about their financial goals is the term "retirement." I'm not saying this goal is wrong, but it's completely generic. Retirement is a generic term that can mean a thousand things to a thousand different people. What exactly do you want "retirement" to look like for you? What age? What lifestyle? Do you want to travel? Volunteer? Be with family?

The key for your financial goals is to make them as specific and personal as possible. Your goals are the reason you will stay on track financially to help you become wealthy. Have fun accomplishing small goals along the way to your bigger goals. Think about not just a "rainy day" fund, but a "joyous day" fund where you can celebrate the excitement of achieving small goals along the journey.

Once you come up with your list of goals, you then need to keep asking yourself the key questions to clarify your goals. Questions can be the best clarifying factor for your goals if you are willing to be honest. Keep "peeling back the onion" to help clarify exactly what you really want. Here is what I mean:

Q: What is your goal?
A: To become a millionaire.

Q: Why do you want to become a millionaire?
A: So, I can retire.

Q: Why do you want to retire?
A: So, I can choose how I spend my time.

Q: Why do you want to choose how you invest your time? (Catch the difference between spend and invest?)
A: So, I can use my time toward the things that matter to me.

Q: What are the things that matter most to you?
A: I want to spend more time with my kids and grand-kids instead of having to work 40+ hours each week for another company.

Q: Why is spending time with family so import-ant to you?
A: They are the people who will remember me most

when I'm gone, and I want to invest my time and energy into them rather than growing a company.

Q: What are the things you would do with your family if you had the time and finances to choose?
A: I would love to take our family each year on an all expenses paid trip to different locations around the world to create memories and give us time to invest in our relationships and teach the values we have to our grandkids so they can pass that on to future generations.

🔒 **WISDOM KEY:**
Find the goal underneath the goal,
and clarify it as much as possible.

Do you see the difference between the first goal of "becoming a millionaire" and the last answer? It could be the same thing because becoming a millionaire allows you to achieve your goal, but no one gets emotional about just becoming a millionaire. People get emotional about what becoming a millionaire could mean to them and their family. Decisions help you start, but discipline helps you finish. Just like your travel plan on vacation can have multiple routes, your financial plan can have multiple routes. Your goals help you stay disciplined through the journey no matter what route you need to take depending on what life throws at you.

You will come across road blocks, slow traffic, and red lights you weren't intending to hit. The key is to keep your end goal in mind so when you eventually hit these road-blocks you can pivot and find another route to your end goal. Always keep your end goals and dreams in front of you at all times. That is what will keep you motivated during the daily grind of life to stay focused on what you really want.

Financial issues are typically one of the top stressors in people's lives. It's typically one of the top (if not the top) reasons couples get divorced. Anything you can do to alleviate this stress will make life better for you and your family long term. It may sound counterintuitive, but having goals outside of yourself is actually very healthy for you as a person. Sanford University lecturer and psychologist Kelly McGonigal wrote a book entitled The *Upside of Stress* in which she states, "people who persistently pursue self-focused goals are more likely to become depressed, while those who pursue bigger-than-self goals show greater well-being and satisfaction with their lives."[1]

My wife sent me this phrasing from a post she saw online from Dave Ramsey and I thought this was so true.

- You will not save money when you get that next raise.
- You will not save money when that car is paid off.
- You will not save money when the kids are grown.
- You will only save money when it becomes an emotional priority.[2]

I couldn't agree with this phrase any more. This is why you have to find your true goal. Only when that goal becomes emotionally important to you will it impact your habits. If your goals don't make an emotional impact on you, you likely haven't found your true goals. Keep going deeper in your goal development until you find a goal that is truly emotionally important to you. That's when your life will change as you pursue something meaningful enough to change how you think about your goals and ultimately change your daily financial habits. The number one reason most people don't get what they want is that they don't know what they really want. Remember that humans are not merely thinking creatures; we are feeling creatures who also think.

Just like when you travel on a physical journey for vacation, distractions constantly arise along the way. You are bombarded with signs of places to stop and spend your hard-earned money and limited time, but you rarely stop on that journey ... why? Your goal is to go to Disneyland; not use your time and money for every promotion you see on a billboard along the way. On your financial journey you will constantly be bombarded with ads and promotions to buy this item or that new gadget. The key is to keep in mind every dollar you use will either help you get to your end goal, or be a distraction along the way.

You will compete with your future millionaire self every single day. You have to decide whether each dollar will HELP you achieve your goals or HURT your progress moving forward. Only you can decide whether that coffee, meal, or clothing purchase is truly necessary. Andy Stanley in his book *Principle of the Path* says, "it's direction-not intention-that determines our destination."[3]

Every purchase steers your financial vehicle in a direction. Make sure each decision is heading in the direction of your end goals.

🔒 WISDOM KEY:
Have a goal that will outlive you and bless those around you.

The mark of true wealth is determined by how much one can give away. When it comes to goals and what you want in life, I hope you take the time to think about how your life and finances can become a legacy that can outlive you. People make a living by what they GET, but they make a life by what they GIVE. No one wants a legacy of being a hoarder. No one wants to be remembered for being a person that lived for themselves. As a former pastor I've been at enough funerals to know that the greatest legacies are the ones where the individual left behind something to bless those behind them.

No one at your funeral will brag about you because of your new car or counter tops. They will brag about you for the blessing you were to them and others. As you come up with your list of goals, I challenge you to have goals that are only for the benefit of others. Ultimately, other people are the ones who will talk about your legacy, good or bad, when you are gone. If your goal doesn't outlive you in some way, shape, or form … it's probably not worth your time chasing. Get a crystal-clear image of a goal that will outlast your life.

As your wealth increases over time, you can either increase your living or increase your giving. Having goals that outlive you is healthy and allows you to keep the focus on things outside of yourself. Have a picture of what "enough" is for you. As your wealth continues to grow, you will have the opportunity to buy more stuff (red light liabilities) or invest those dollars to bless the people around you. No one will care about the cars, boats, or square footage of your home.

Your legacy will be determined by how you impacted others. As part of your long-term goals, have boundaries for what "enough" is and make a conscious choice to increase your giving instead of your living as you develop wealth. Your decisions never affect just you. When you say "yes" or "no" it will always impact others in some way, sometimes in big ways we never thought possible.

You need to be a student of yourself and your financial habits. Everyone has strengths and weaknesses when it comes to how they spend and invest their funds. What areas are weaknesses for you? Clothing? Eating out? Daily coffees? Entertainment? Cars? Hunting gear (sorry guys, had to throw that one in there)? If you are tempted late at night to buy random items while scrolling on your phone, maybe you should set a daily alarm for a certain time (8 p.m.) to get off the screen and read a book. If you are tempted on the way home to stop by the casino or go through the drive-through again, maybe have a picture of your true financial goals in your vehicle to remind you of what you really want.

This is why having a picture of your true financial goal is so important. That goal is what helps motivate you to get through the daily battle of stopping at financial "red lights" that keep you from becoming wealthy. Know your weaknesses and build guardrails around them to keep you focused.

All you have to do is look through your checkbook or monthly transactions to see what your true priority is. If you spend more money on eating out and entertainment than you do investing for your future, you know what your priorities are. You don't have to tell others your goals; your goals are clearly stated in your spending habits.

Quit lying to yourself that retirement, giving generously, or becoming a millionaire are your top goals when you spend more money on pizza and coffee than you invest in yourself and your family's future. Your goals will drive every dollar you invest. Take a look at each dollar and ensure each dollar is pointing toward a goal. Becoming a "Green Light Millionaire" is not just about money; it's about becoming wise in how you think and steward your resources. What you get by reaching your goals is not nearly as important as what you become by reaching them.

Long term you want to increase the percentage of your income you invest every year. I have my own kids invest 10 percent of their money into long term investments to teach them the principle that paying themselves first must be a top priority over paying for lifestyle choices. Our kids have three jars (Give, Save, Spend). With every dollar they earn they put 10 percent in Give (this is first), 10 percent into Save (they pay their future selves before paying a store for their lifestyle), and 80 percent into Spend. This is very basic but anyone can use this simple give, save, spend example, and then your goal is to increase your giving and saving long term. As you no longer have as many liabilities (red lights) and have more assets (green lights), you have more cash flow to allow you to increase your giving and investing to grow your net worth for decades to come.

Be sure to also set annual financial goals that help point toward your long-term goals. My wife and I set financial goals every year, and part of our goal-setting also includes giving. This way we can come back to the smaller annual goal to help us stay focused on the long-term goals. Take time every year to set smaller goals that keep you focused on the long-term goals.

🔒 WISDOM KEY:

Comparison is the root of all unhappiness.

Just like when you go on a trip, you visit places and have experiences unique to you and your family. What may be a goal for someone else may not mean anything to you. Stop comparing your goals and lifestyle to those around you. If you base your success on competing with other people's highlight reels, you will always lose at the end of the day.

Every time you compare, you create a loser. Have you ever thought of that? Either you lose or the other person loses, but when you have goals based on what others are doing, someone always loses. Your life can't compete with the highlight on someone else's social media. Stay focused on your dreams and goals, and ensure every dollar points toward that end goal to help hit every possible green light to achieve that goal as quickly and effectively as possible.

I know it can be hard for many of us to figure out what our

true goals are. Beyond asking yourself deeper questions, use this simple key to setting goals for yourself: SMART Goals.

S—Specific: Make your goals as specific in detail as possible. You want the goal to draw out emotion to push you toward putting your hard-earned dollars toward assets (green lights) and not liabilities (red lights).

M—Measurable: This helps you determine if you are on track. You can measure how much money you invest each month toward your future goals.

A—Achievable: Make sure your goals are realistic and achievable. If you currently have a net worth of $0 and earn $50,000/year, don't set a goal of having a net worth of $1,000,000 in one year. Remember, things that are built to last are usually not built fast.

R—Relevant: Ensure every goal aligns with your values and long-term plans. If the goal doesn't point toward a deeply personal vision for your life, achieving that goal likely isn't relevant to you at the end of the day.

T—Time-bound: Set clear timelines for each goal with a clear end date so you can see if you are on track to achieve the goal by a certain timeline.

Allow your goals to be flexible. Your desires will likely change over time and that is okay. What you want to achieve in your thirties may differ from when you get to your mid- to late-fifties. Always keep your goals in front of you at all times and give yourself permission to add/adjust/remove goals as you move toward your long-term financial goals. Maybe you take on a new hobby in your forties that you want to invest your time in, or maybe kids move farther away or closer to you and you want more time with kids and grandkids.

Be flexible as you move along, but always ensure that every dollar is properly stewarded and strategically invested toward the goals you pursue. If you don't have a crystal-clear picture of your goals, it's very easy to hit a bunch of extra red lights (liabilities) along your journey that slow down your ability to achieve the things that are truly important to you.

To achieve a goal you have never achieved before, you must start doing things you have never done before. As you start to accomplish your goals, you will want to constantly update your list of goals to continue to challenge and grow yourself long term. Always be adding to the list of goals.

Find goals that are beyond yourself to bless those around you; not just your immediate family, but your church, your community and the world around you. Allow your goals to keep adjusting over time. This helps keep you motivated to always be willing to step outside of your comfort zone and grow in the impact you can have through your finances as you develop more and more wealth long term.

CHAPTER 7

YOUR FIRST $100,000

The Hardest Part of Building Assets to Become a Millionaire

Joe Wealthy understood the power of compounding interest. Every dollar he and his family put aside helped them gain more future momentum. Instead of getting coffees daily and buying the latest fashion trend, Joe chose to live well within his means and invest for his long-term goals. The first years weren't impressive. In fact, Joe actually saw his assets drop in value the first year when the market dropped. Joe kept his composure and kept investing every month for his goals. A 10 percent return on $1,000 in the early days was only $100, which did not seem much at the time. Now Joe's net worth is over $1,000,000, and a 10 percent return grows his net worth substantially. The early years were a struggle to see a couple hundred dollars growth from his assets, but now that debts are paid down and his assets are working on his behalf, Joe's net worth can grow by six figures without him even doing anything.

Ben Broke also understood the power of compounding interest. Unfortunately for Ben, when he saw only a couple of hundred dollars of growth early on in his account, he decided it wasn't worth his time and stopped contributing when he was younger. Ben also chose to buy coffees, ate out constantly, and took out loans for new vehicles, which also worked against his ability to grow assets that could compound for him. Now the Broke family has little traction from their assets because they are much smaller than they should be. Ben was encouraged when he saw his investment account jump a couple thousand dollars, but he feared it may be too little too late as he still has few assets that can provide for his future. Ben now sees the importance of letting his assets pay for his liabilities, but he still loses focus when the newer model vehicle comes out, they see new furniture, or when it's time to plan the family meals instead of eating out at the last minute. Ben now can only wish he would have started properly investing years earlier to get past that first $100,000 in net worth.

When it comes to being successful in any area of life, most of the friction is usually at the beginning of the journey. Whether you are starting a business or investing for retirement, the first steps never feel that great and can feel pointless when looked at in light of your end goal. This is why this chapter follows the chapter on goals. The beginning stages of wealth development are typically the hardest. Building wealth is a long-term play, but it can't be a long-term delay.

Getting yourself to think like a millionaire takes time, and the first steps are usually the longest and hardest to take. Just like the debt snowball from chapter three can start off slow, the investment snowball will likely start off slow. Just be patient, and the true rewards of wealth development will come with time and consistency. Trust me, the investment snowball is a lot more fun than the debt snowball!

This shouldn't come as a surprise that the first steps are the toughest. This is true for almost any area of life. Think about all the people who make New Year's resolutions. Various sources say around 80 to 90 percent of New Year's resolutions are broken by the second week in February. In fact, the second Friday of January is now referred to as "quitter's day" because so many people have given up on their goals by then. Why? Because those first steps are the hardest. Those pounds you are trying to lose don't come off as fast as you want. The notches on your belt don't tighten as fast as you desired. That's why the focus of this book is not about a specific way to become wealthy. To change your habits, you first have to change the way you think. Your thinking is key to getting past the first hurdles to obtaining your first $100,000 of net worth.

Yes, those first dollars may seem small and insignificant. Yes, it takes intentionality to think about each dollar as a seed to be planted (invested) or thrown out (spent). Maybe the visual of the stoplight doesn't connect with you as much, but maybe you need to think about each dollar that leaves your hand like a seed. Every seed (dollar) planted has the potential to create huge rewards in the long run. Every time you destroy a financial seed by throwing it away toward liabilities is a future tree that just died. If you want to be able to relax in the shade in future years and take it easy, you will have to put in the work now to plant those seeds into your financial assets that can provide protection of your goals long term.

🔒 **WISDOM KEY:**

Track Net worth annually to provide guidance on your progress.

Net worth is a simple tracking tool to help keep a gauge on whether you are winning or losing when it comes to wealth development. Think of tracking your net worth like stepping on a scale. It is a snapshot in time of your financial health. While there is much more to tracking your physical health than stepping on a scale, there is also much more to your financial health than just your overall net worth. What the net worth allows you to track is how well you are making progress each year. NOTE—Don't track net worth each month as accounts can fluctuate. Your time and energy are better spent focused on principles to develop wealth.

Don't feel down if your net worth decreases from one year to the next if there is a market crash and your accounts are lower. Just stay focused on the principles of putting your money toward assets (green lights) that will help grow your net worth and help you develop wealth over time. Small steps are far better than great intentions.

Again, definitions are important. Your bank will give you a net worth statement that will include vehicle and other household items to add to your net worth. If the item is not helping you make money ... IT IS NOT AN ASSET!

First, list the assets you own in a column and total up the value to give you a total number. It's fine if you want to include your personal residence to just track net worth as you do have equity in your home, but remember your personal residence will not be a financial asset for your wealth development. You may want to list your 'qualified assets' (401(k), IRA, 403(b), Roth IRA) in its own column to help track tax efficiencies (see example below).

Second, list any items that are debts in a separate column and get a total number. Once you have both numbers take your total assets and minus your debts. This is your net worth that you can track moving forward to give you an annual visual to check if you are heading in the right direction.

Ultimately, your goal should be to build up assets and become a millionaire outside of your personal residence. AKA—Green Light Millionaire.

EXAMPLE - NET WORTH SPREADSHEET FOR JOHN AND JANE DOE

Non-Qualified Assets	Amount	Qualified Assets	Amount	Liabilities	Amount
Home	$500,000	John - 401(k)	$200,000	Mortgage	$385,000
Checking	$5,000	Jane - 403(b)	$150,000	Rental Mortgage	$300,000
Savings	$15,000	John - IRA	$25,000	Vehicle	$40,000
Joint Brokerage	$25,000	Jane - Roth IRA	$75,000	School Loans	$60,000
Rental Property	$400,000	John old 401(k)	$150,000	Credit Card	$25,000
TOTAL	$945,000	**TOTAL**	$600,000	**TOTAL**	$810,000

Total Assets	$1,545,000
Total Liabilities	$810,000
NET WORTH (including home)	**$735,000**

🔒 **WISDOM KEY:**

Compounding interest is king.

Compounding interest can either be your best friend or your worst enemy when it comes to wealth development. If you have debts, you have things (red lights) that work against you every single month to hinder your wealth development. Your assets over time can compound on themselves to help you create more wealth, which eventually gives you more options to choose what you want to do long term.

Money can either be a terrible master or a wonderful servant. If you can get money to work for you, it will serve you and your goals well, like a faithful servant. If your money is used for debts and lifestyle, it will be a horrible master that you will serve instead of your money serving you and your goals. The earlier you can start building your assets, the better. Don't wait to buy assets; buy assets and wait!

Stay with me for the next couple of examples. I know numbers aren't exciting, but the following examples show the power of how compound interest can work for you.

EXAMPLE 1:

Investing $10,000 vs putting $10,000 on credit cards and making minimum payments.

GOOD (green light) example: You invest $10,000 (green light asset) and let it grow for you at 7.2 percent a year. You would have doubled the size of this asset in ten years without adding anything else to it. (SEE CHART BELOW)

Year	Balance	Interest Earned	End Balance
1	$10,000.00	$720.00	$10,720.00
2	$10,720.00	$771.84	$11,491.84
3	$11,491.84	$827.41	$12,319.25
4	$12,319.25	$886.99	$13,206.24
5	$13,206.24	$950.85	$14,154.09
6	$14,154.09	$1,019.31	$15,176.40
7	$15,176.40	$1,092.70	$16,269.10
8	$16,269.10	$1,171.38	$17,440.47
9	$17,440.47	$1,255.71	$18,696.19
10	$18,696.19	$1,346.13	$20,042.31[1]

---

[1] This is a hypothetical example that is demonstrating a mathematical principle. It does not illustrate any investment products and does not show past or future performance of any specific investment.

BAD (red light) example: Putting $10,000 on a credit card to pay for a family vacation.

You put $10,000 on a credit card with 23.4 percent interest to pay for your Disneyland vacation, and you make minimum payments of $200/month. You would need to pay on this credit card for SIXTEEN YEARS, and the total cost would be $38,202. That's an additional $28,202 in red light expenses, which is almost a $50,000 cost in comparison to investing $10,000 in the green light example. The debt is like putting on the parking brake on your financial vehicle. You can't expect to move forward with a parking brake on. Get rid of that as soon as possible. Making minimum payments ensures you will hit as many red lights as possible.

(SEE CHART BELOW FOR RED LIGHT EXAMPLE)

End of Year	CC Balance	Interest Paid	Total cost of payments
1	$9,939.31	$2,339.31	$2,400
4	$9,608.49	$9,208.49	$9,600
8	$8,619.18	$17,819.18	$19,200
12	$6,119.31	$24,919.31	$28,800
16	$0.00	$28,202.38	$38,202.38

These may seem like extreme examples, but a 7.2 percent interest rate is reasonable to earn on your investment assets, and $10,000 is not an extreme example in today's society. These examples are to help you understand how compounding interest can be a blessing or a burden in developing wealth.

Look at the first line of the green light example. The gain is only $720/year on that account, but in ten years that gain becomes over $1,300/year just in interest. This is where the wealthy use their assets to pay for their liabilities. The financially poor continue to make purchases monthly through their income instead of building assets. The wealthy continue to build their assets, which buys them the things they really want long term.

So why is the first $100,000 of net worth the hardest? Let's say you have no assets currently and decide to invest $10,000/year that will earn 7 percent interest. You would have a net worth of $100,000 in less than eight years. Basically, it took you almost eight years to get to $100,000 of net worth. Now let's fast forward your wealth development to a net worth of $900,000 in assets that earn that same 7 percent. Now you will gain $100,000 in net worth in less than one- and-a-half years. Your ability to grow your net worth of $100,000 is almost five times faster from $900,000 to $1,000,000 as it was from $0 to $100,000.

Also, keep in mind that the growth from $900,000 to a MILLION is only on the interest your assets have earned. You were no longer adding funds in that example. This is the massive power of compounding interest and why the first $100,000 is so vital to get as quickly as possible. The quicker you build up your assets (green lights), the quicker those assets can work on your behalf to speed up your financial journey. You have to force yourself to pay yourself first before you pay for your lifestyle.

EXAMPLE 2:

Growing net worth by $100,000 (assuming 7% growth rate).

	Current	Future
Start net worth	$0	$900,000
Additions	$10,000/year	NONE
Years to grow $100,000 net worth	7.84 years	1.35 years
End net worth	$100,000	$1,000,000

This is why when you hear people discuss investing every day instead of stopping by "Sevenbucks" (sorry, bad play on words for wasting money on your caffeinated beverage), you know why those purchases make a huge difference in the long run. It's the first steps that are the hardest. It's the first $100,000 that takes the most friction to get your momentum of wealth development going. In the example of going from $900,000 to $1,000,000, you are growing your net worth, and the growth can pay for all those beverages in the future.

Now every time you think about going through the drive-through or ordering something on your phone app, you can mentally decide whether this is a green light to achieve your financial goals or if this is a red light that will keep you financially struggling. As Dave Ramsey is famous for saying, keep that gazelle-like intensity to achieve your goals (especially those first steps). If you live like no one else today you can live and give like no one else in the future. Red light vs green light financial decisions will decide how quickly you get that first $100,000. Remember, the secret of your success is hidden in your daily routine. Wealth develops daily, not in a day.

We all make mistakes on our financial journey. Some just make them more often. Millionaires do daily (invest in green lights) what poor people do occasionally. When you trip up, just make sure that mistake is a stepping stone to learn from and not a stopping stone you dwell on. That $7 coffee can make a difference in the long run as it's the minor adjustments that lead to major success. It may take time to get used to these new financial decisions.

Good habits are difficult to acquire, but easy to live with long term. Bad habits are easy to acquire, but difficult to live with long term. You get to decide today what your habits will be. Remember, the difference between a financial chump and a financial champ is the little extra effort to get over the hump to turn your "u" into an "a."

A classic TV sitcom, *The Office*, has useful insight. In

episode 16 of season three, the Branch Manager Michael Scott looks at his employee, Dwight Schrute, and asks, "What is the most inspiring thing I have ever said to you?" Dwight replies by saying, "'Don't be an idiot. Changed my life." Dwight goes on to say in his own monologue, "Whenever I'm about to do something I think, 'Would an idiot do that?' And if they would, I do not do that thing."[1] Maybe this question can help when you consider how you are going to steward your next dollar. If a financial idiot would do that … don't do that thing.

Financial idiots rob from their future selves to pay for today's lifestyle. Financial idiots swipe credit cards instead of investing in their retirement accounts. Financial idiots spend money on red light purchases instead of investing in themselves. Every purchase you make that is a financial liability (red light) steals from yourself at some point in the future. Are you ready to stop being a financial idiot and quit stealing from yourself?

CHAPTER 8

MENTORSHIP

Why You Need Others
Along the Journey

Joe Wealthy is a busy man and understood the need to have his time and energy focused on his work, family, volunteering, and other things important to him. Since he first started investing, he had others come alongside him in his journey. Thankfully when he lost money during the first year investing, his financial advisor told him to stay the course and not sell off his investments. He now has a tax advisor and estate planning attorney on his team to help him properly plan for his wealth/estate transfer strategy. Joe knows that to help him stay wealthy, he needs others who can constantly watch his investments and ensure his taxes remain as low as possible. Joe has seen the videos online with the get-rich-quick advice, but thankfully Joe continues to do the little things that have compounded for him through the advice he gets from his team to continue to grow wealth.

Ben Broke also lost money early on when he started investing. Instead of listening to his advisor at the time, he pulled all his money out of his investments. He invested randomly since then and based decisions on advice from coworkers or online videos. Unfortunately, Ben did more speculating than investing. He hoped each investment would return huge gains for him as he only invested at random times outside of his employer retirement plan. Ben thought that doing this on his own was best, so he didn't have anyone helping him with investments, taxes, or estate planning. Ultimately, this showed itself in the fact that Ben doesn't really have a financial plan in place. He implemented random ideas that came his way, but there was no focused plan to achieve his goals. This strategy (or lack of strategy) caused Ben to fall behind financially and have a much lower net worth than those who made much less than him.

We have been using the analogy of traveling on a journey when it comes to helping you develop wealth to become a millionaire and achieve your financial goals. Think about any kind of long trip you have taken in the past. When you map out your plan, you are using an app (or apps) to help you arrive at your final destination. You don't just start driving and hope you can make it. You put your trust in a team of developers who have put in the time and energy to develop a software that helps you navigate the turns and roadblocks you face. You put your trust in a team at a hotel, Airbnb, or campground for your lodging, and you navigate where to stop for meals and rest breaks to ensure you enjoy the entire trip. Even a simple idea of a vacation takes many others to help you put everything together.

The same holds true for your financial journey. There are so many potential roadblocks and efficiencies that can easily get missed that you will want others who can assist with all the various questions that can come up. Even as a CERTIFIED FINANCIAL PLANNER™ (CFP®), I utilize other experts in our field of financial planning, estate planning, and tax planning to ensure nothing gets missed with my personal financial plan and the financial plans for our clients.

You should have at least three people in your corner when it comes to your financial journey: 1) financial planner who can help coordinate a plan, 2) tax advisor who can ensure you are taking advantage of every tax break you can get, and 3) estate planning attorney who can ensure your overall estate transfer strategy is legally put together. No one person can be an expert in every area. Just like in a football game the quarterback gets a lot of attention, but in almost every play he needs to hand the ball off or pass the ball to someone else on the team. The same is true for you moving forward as you become a Green Light Millionaire.

You should have people in every area of your life that are helping you become better every day. Whether it's with your finances, faith, family, fitness, or career, you need others to grow and challenge you to get better. You don't have the time or energy to be an expert in every area. The good news is there are others who are experts in certain areas who can assist you. This could be a personal trainer for your fitness, a pastor or trusted spiritual leader for your faith, or someone who can guide you in your career or business venture.

Don't get caught up in your pride to think you know it all. Be humble and always be teachable as long as you live. Too many people think that once they graduate school, they are finished learning. The reality is that if you aren't growing you are dying, and that is true no matter whether you talk about finance, faith, or any other area of life.

The good news is that mentorship at a high level doesn't take much effort. Whether it's a book (like the one you are reading), podcast, or conference, there are many great resources to help you take those first steps on your journey. But eventually you will want people who can come alongside you. You will want someone who can mentor you and give you guidance to reach the next level of your wealth development. Just like you want to learn from others to be physically healthy, you want to be able to learn from others who are financially healthy as well.

🔒 **WISDOM KEY:**

Never take advice from someone who doesn't have what you want.

This is where financial mentorship is hard. People can appear successful from the outside. It's easy to follow a YouTuber because they have videos in front of an expensive car. It's easy to follow a podcaster because they have some nice quotes, but is the advice you are getting based on sound financial principles? Be cautious of someone trying to sell some get-rich-quick gimmick or easy path to financial success. The road to success is not easy, and it usually looks like hard work.

If you really look behind the curtain at most people in America, you will find that those with the expensive homes and cars are not the wealthy. They are the ones with the highest monthly payments. Read the classic book by Thomas J. Stanley, *The Millionaire Next Door: The Surprising Secrets of America's Wealthy* for more details on this or the follow-up, *The Next Millionaire Next Door* written by Thomas Stanley and Sarah Stanley Fallaw.

Be cautious of the "free" advice you get from coworkers, neighbors, family, or friends. They likely have good intentions and may potentially have great insight, but do they have a life you want to live? Remember, sometimes "free" advice can cost the most in the end.

For business owners, this can definitely become a challenge. While financial advice can apply to anyone in any field, you may have a business in which you need specific insight in how to be successful. Again, swallow your pride and find people in your field whom you can ask questions of to learn from their mistakes instead of making your own. Whether you own a restaurant, manufacturing company, multi-level marketing (MLM) company, retail store, or any other business, you want and need others to help guide you on your journey to wealth development.

There is no single route to becoming a millionaire, but once you figure out which route to take for your career, do everything you can to get others around you as quickly as possible to help guide you toward success in that field. There are some "expenses" that are green light purchases for a business to grow and expand. This is also why mentorship is key for business owners as each market your business serves is so unique that you can get high-level insights from a book, but eventually you want and need others to mentor you directly.

🔒 WISDOM KEY:

The best investment you can make ... is in yourself.

The fastest way to get rich and stay rich is to work on developing you. If you want to be successful long term, you have to be investing for the rest of your life. Don't get caught in the trap of being able to "coast through life." Your life doesn't work that way. If you aren't working your physical body constantly, you slowly get more and more out of shape. If you don't invest in your marriage and close relationships, they will slowly fall apart.

For those who can only afford to invest a very small ($50/month) it may be your best option to invest that $50 into yourself in the form of books (like the one you are reading), seminars, or courses that can help you be more marketable or knowledgeable to be successful long term. Let's say you do this for a year and spend $600. Then this investment into yourself then helps you increase your earnings by $1,000/month. You just made a huge return on your money by investing in yourself which gives you more income earning potential to invest long term.

You are your greatest green light asset.

If you aren't growing, you are dying, and that rule applies to all areas of your life. If you don't challenge yourself mentally to grow and think better, you will slowly fall into coasting into average, which will leave you broke. The people in your life that you should envy are the ones who are still working to achieve a goal in all areas of their lives. Never stop investing in yourself to become the best version of you that you can be. If you are through learning, you're through.

Just like you read in the chapter about the first $100,000 being the hardest, the same is true for you in your life. Yes, I want you to become financially wealthy and be a millionaire. But if you become wealthy and have terrible relationships with your family and terrible physical health because you never exercised or ate correctly, will it be worth it? No way! Just like the compounding of interest in your finances takes time, so does the compounding effect of the mentors you put around you.

Having a financial advisor doesn't mean you will be a millionaire in a week (although that would be great), and just because you hire a personal trainer doesn't mean you will have a six-pack in less than a month (that may be even better than being a millionaire in a week). Mentorship and learning take time, and they compound as you continue to learn and challenge yourself to become better.

Rich people constantly learn and grow, poor people think they already know. You may think you are smart enough to take this journey on your own, but you are likely taking a small sample size when it comes to any proper comparison of your overall financial journey. Just like the dad who starts his family vacation by getting on the correct interstate, he would be a fool to think he could go the entire way without any other input. The same goes for you and your financial journey ... eventually there may be turns or detours, and you will need other resources to guide you.

Just because you picked a single stock in your Robin-hood account, or timed the market right when maxing out your Roth IRA one year, doesn't mean you should fly solo the rest of the journey. Your goals, risk tolerances, and time horizons can change over time, and you will want others who can help you navigate those changes.

I was an exercise science major when I first went to college and know a fair amount about health and fitness, but I'm still wise enough to work with a nutritionist on a consistent basis to ensure my diet is dialed in. The same principle applies to any area of life, and that includes finances.

Vanguard put out statistics of the value that clients get when working with someone like a financial advisor. Most people know Vanguard as the inexpensive guy on the block with low-cost investment options, so for them to come out with this should make you take notice. They added up the value that the advisor could provide in areas of rebalancing, asset allocation, behavioral coaching, and spending strategy (withdrawal order in retirement), and according to their numbers stated the value of having assistance can reach 3 percent (or more) difference in the long run.[1]

Yes, you can go and pick an ETF or single stock. You can go and invest in a business or buy some real estate. Just make sure you have trusted advisors in any of these areas who can guide you. Even just a 1 percent difference in the long run helps those green light assets build up significantly more over time, and mentorship can help make that happen faster for you. The key to lifelong learning is feedback. It is nearly impossible to learn anything without it. Just remain teachable your entire life.

My hope is this book can provide a little insight into thinking of your finances differently. Maybe a simple concept of thinking red light vs. green light can help you start to think differently about every dollar that comes across your bank account. No one has the capacity to personally mentor thousands of people, but hopefully through this book and the ideas and thoughts presented, it can help you start or further your journey to achieve the financial goals you have for you and your family.

Ultimately you have to put these principles in place for yourself. You have to choose to make different financial decisions in order to change the trajectory for your family. You have to spend time figuring out your true goals and desires. No one else can do that for you. Mentors can help provide guidance and insight and are an integral part of the journey, but you still have to choose to put mentors in place. You were not designed to go through life alone. You were designed to take this life journey with others. Make sure you put people around you to help you become successful in every area of life!

CHAPTER 9

WEALTH DEVELOPMENT

Stewardship, the Key to Lifelong Financial Success

Joe Wealthy has understood the importance of wealth development and stewardship his whole life. Grateful for the influence of others who have guided him, Joe understands that he came into the world with nothing and he won't take anything with him when his life is over. Since all he has is temporarily in his hands, he wants to be as wise as possible his entire life. No matter if Joe is eighteen years old or eighty-eight years old, he understands the need to ensure every dollar that comes into his possession is properly utilized. This mindset helps Joe understand there is no "end" to his financial journey while he is alive. He knows he will need to properly steward and invest his entire life to help him achieve his generosity and estate planning goals as well as set the example for his kids and grandkids on how to properly utilize the resources they will one day be responsible for.

Ben Broke continues to simply live for the moment. He holds onto each of his possessions with great intensity to ensure he doesn't lose a grasp on what he considers his possessions. Ben has lost sight of the fact that he came into this world with nothing and will also leave with nothing. Ben also keeps thinking that proper wealth development and stewardship is something you only do later in life. Ben failed to understand that development and stewardship never end. Even though Ben should have started sooner, he could still start today with properly stewarding and developing his wealth. Ben also fails to realize that his children are watching his financial patterns and are not aware they should be stewarding their own dollars and begin their wealth development journey. Ben hopes to pass down money to his kids, but even if he does, if they don't understand proper wealth development and stewardship principles it won't matter. Ben's children and grandchildren may likely follow his example as the family stays broke for generations to come. Ben wants to start now to set an appropriate example for his kids and grandkids to follow. He wants to teach them that wealth development and stewardship are a never-ending process.

As you close out this book, I believe this chapter will ultimately be the most important part of your financial journey. The reality is when you came into this world, you had nothing and you will leave this world the same way. You may have heard the humorous phrase that "You will never see a hearse pulling a U-Haul." While we can smile at that phrase, it should humble us to know that it's true. Part of this last section will reference goals, but it's ultimately about understanding where your wealth comes from and how you can use that wealth not just for yourself but your family, church, charities, and community to bless those around you.

When you take a family road trip, the journey isn't about you. It's about the others in your vehicle and the things you want them to experience. Yes, you can (and should) enjoy the journey as well, and the journey should be a blessing to those who are traveling, but you don't invest all the time and energy for a family vacation to Disney for your kids and family to have a miserable time. You are trying to steward the moments on behalf of your family to have the greatest experience possible along the way.

As a CERTIFIED FINANCIAL PLANNER™ (CFP®), I

work with hundreds of families a year, helping them develop their strategies to develop their wealth. We work with millionaires on a weekly basis who want every dollar to be strategically allocated to each of their goals. I've worked with couples who make a combined income well over $250,000/year who have a negative net worth, and I've worked with couples making a combined income of less than $100,000/year who have a seven-figure net worth. Why? Because as we have discussed, it doesn't matter how much you make. It matters how much you keep to invest. The families with a seven- and eight-figure net worth understand they need to put their money into assets that can grow their net worth for years and decades to come.

🔒 **WISDOM KEY:**

Stewardship never ends, it's a lifelong pursuit.

Stewardship is a unique term in today's culture that is not used often, and maybe this is why our culture has so many financial problems to begin with. Stewardship is simply understanding what we have is not our own, and that means we manage that resource (in this case money) on behalf of someone else. We brought no money into the world when we were born, and we will leave this world with nothing as well. Properly understanding the ownership helps us steward every dollar we have for purposes greater than ourselves.

Whether you are reading this book and you are eighteen years old or eighty-eight years old, you have the choice today and, in the future, to steward every dollar you have wisely. At the end of your life here on earth you won't be remembered for the size of your net worth or the assets in your possession. Yes, those things are important as you want to steward your finances wisely, but your legacy will ultimately be what you did for others.

Your nice car, boat, vacation home, clothes, and other possessions will get sold off when you die. It's the relationships and causes you invest in that will outlast your time here on earth. Developing wealth isn't just about money. You can be wealthy with relationships and influence, and that wealth is worth way more than any investment account you will ever have.

As a former pastor I've been a part of many end-of-life situations with people and I've never heard anyone on their deathbed brag about being a millionaire or talk about their possessions. The end of the journey always focuses on relationships and the experiences along the way.

🔒 WISDOM KEY:
Pass on financial wisdom, not just financial wealth.

Yes, you should wisely steward every dollar you have. Yes, you should take care of your family financially and set up the next generation for success. Just remember that wealth development is not just a financial conversation. While finances impact almost every area of life, there is much more to your life than becoming a millionaire.

The principles you read about in this book all came from a book people know as the Bible. The good news for anyone reading this is that the principles in this book apply to anyone whether you follow Jesus or not. You can be an atheist and apply these principles and become very wealthy. You can be a Christian and not apply these principles and stay in financial poverty your whole life. The principles are universal to anyone who chooses to implement them. Your path to wealth development and becoming a millionaire will look different than others, but the principles are timeless and can impact your life and change the direction of your family for generations to come.

Allow me to show you that each of these core principles discussed have a foundation that isn't based on market fluctuations or how a certain industry will do. It's based on God's Word, which does not change. You want to build a foundation for you and your family that can adjust to roadblocks and detours as you develop your wealth and become a millionaire. Your financial journey needs to have a foundation of something that will not change over time.

2 Timothy 3:16-17 (NLV) says, "All Scripture is inspired by God and is useful to teach us what is true and to make us realize what is wrong in our lives. It corrects us when we are wrong and teaches us to do what is right. God uses it to prepare and equip His people to do every good work." Here is a list of Bible verses that provide the foundation for each chapter of the book:

Chapter 1: Introduction
(Importance of proper thinking and being teachable)

Proverbs 18:13 *(NLT)—Spouting off before listening to the facts is both shameful and foolish.*

Proverbs 13:18 *(NLT)—If you ignore criticism, you will end in poverty and disgrace; if you accept correction, you will be honored.*

2 Timothy 3:16 *(NLT) —All Scripture is inspired by God and is useful to teach us what is true and to make us realize what is wrong in our lives. It corrects us when we are wrong and teaches us to do what is right.*

Colossians 3:16 *(The Message Bible)— Let the Word of Christ— the Message—have the run of the house. Give it plenty of room in your lives. Instruct and direct one another using good common sense.*

Chapter 2: Assets (Green Lights)

Proverbs 21:20 *(ESV)—Precious treasure and oil are in a wise man's dwelling, but a foolish man devours it.*

Proverbs 13:11 *(ESV)—Wealth gained hastily will dwindle, but whoever gathers little by little will increase it.*

Ecclesiastes 11:2 *(NLT)—But divide your investments among many places, for you do not know what risks might lie ahead.*

2 Corinthians 9:6 *(NIV)—Remember this: Whoever sows sparingly will also reap sparingly, and whoever sows generously will also reap generously.*

Proverbs 16:8 *(Good News Translation)—It is better to have a little, honestly earned, than to have a large income, dishonestly gained.*

1 Timothy 3:5 *(NLT) - For if a man cannot manage his own household, how can he take care of God's church?*

Deuteronomy 8:18 *(NIV)—But remember the Lord your God, for it is he who gives you the ability to produce wealth, and so confirms his covenant, which he swore to your ancestors, as it is today.*

Chapter 3: Liabilities (Red Lights)

Proverbs 22:7 *(ESV)—The rich rules over the poor, and the borrower is slave to the lender.*

Romans 13:8 *(NASB)—Owe nothing to anyone except to love one another; for the one who loves his neighbor has fulfilled the law.*

Proverbs 17:18 *(The Message Bible)—It's stupid to try to get something for nothing, or run up huge bills you can never pay.*

Luke 12:15 *(NIV)—Then he (Jesus) said to them, "Watch out! Be on your guard against all kinds of greed; life does not consist in an abundance of possessions."*

Ecclesiastes 5:5 *(NIV)—It is better not to make a vow than to make one and not fulfill it.*

Proverbs 12:9 *(NLT)—Better to be an ordinary person with a servant than to be self-important but have no food.*

Chapter 4: Personal Home (Yellow Lights)

Proverbs 24:27 *(NLT)—Do your planning and prepare your fields before building your house.*

Proverbs 24:3-4 *(NLT)—A house is built by wisdom and becomes strong through good sense. Through knowledge its rooms are filled with all sorts of precious riches and valuables.*

Jeremiah 29:5 *(ESV)—Build houses and live in them; plant gardens and eat their produce.*

Numbers 33:53 *(NIV)—Take possession of the land and settle in it, for I have given you the land to possess.*

2 Corinthians 5:1 *(NASB)—For we know that if the earthly tent which is our house is torn down, we have a building from God, a house not made with hands, eternal in the heavens.*

Chapter 6: Goals

Proverbs 29:18 *(Legacy Standard Bible)—Where there is no vision, the people are out of control, But how blessed is he who keeps the law.*

2 Chronicles 15:7 *(ESV)—But you, take courage! Do not let your hands be weak, for your work shall be rewarded.*

Luke 12:15 *(NIV)—Then he said to them, "Watch out! Be on your guard against all kinds of greed; life does not consist in an abundance of possessions."*

Proverbs 21:5 *(NIV)—The plans of the diligent lead to profit as surely as haste leads to poverty.*

Philippians 4:8 *(NIV)—Finally, brothers and sisters, whatever is true, whatever is noble, whatever is right, whatever is pure, whatever is lovely, whatever is admirable - if anything is excellent or praiseworthy - think about such things.*

Proverbs 16:9 *(NASB)—The mind of man plans his way, But the Lord directs his steps.*

1 Corinthians 2:9 *(NLT)—No eye has seen, no ear has heard, and no mind has imagined what God has prepared for those who love him.*

Chapter 8: Mentorship

Proverbs 15:22 *(The Message)—Refuse good advice and watch your plans fail; take good counsel and watch them succeed.*

Proverbs 17:16 *(NLT)—It is senseless to pay to educate a fool, since he has no heart for learning.*

Proverbs 27:17 *(ESV)—Iron sharpens iron, and one man sharpens another.*

Proverbs 13:20 *(The Message Bible)—Become wise by walking with the wise; hang out with fools and watch your life fall to pieces.*

Proverb 9:9 *(Contemporary English Version)—If you have good sense, instruction will help you to have even better sense. And if you live right, education will help you to know even more.*

Psalm 119:130 *(NLT)—The teaching of your word gives light, so even the simple can understand.*

Proverbs 14:7 *(NLT)—Stay away from fools, for you won't find knowledge on their lips.*

Proverbs 14:15 *(GNT)—A fool will believe anything; smart people watch their step.*

Proverbs 3:5-6 *(NIV)—Trust in the Lord with all your heart and lean not on your own understanding; in all your ways submit to him, and he will make your paths straight.*

Chapter 9: Wealth Development (Stewardship)

Psalm 24:1 *(NIV)—The earth is the Lord's, and everything in it, the world, and all who live in it.*

Genesis 2:15 *(NASB)—Then the Lord took the man and put him into the garden of Eden to cultivate it and keep it.*

Colossians 3:23 *(NIV)—Whatever you do, work at it with all your heart, as working for the Lord, not for human masters.*

1 Corinthians 4:2 *(ESV)—Moreover, it is required of stewards that they be found faithful.*

Matthew 6:20 *(ESV)—But lay up for yourselves treasures in heaven, where neither moth nor rust destroys and where thieves do not break in and steal.*

John 6:27 *(NIV)—Do not work for food that spoils, but for food that endures to eternal life, which the Son of Man will give you. For on him God the Father has placed his seal of approval.*

Mark 8:36 *(NLT)—And what do you benefit if you gain the whole world but lose your own soul?*

Matthew 25:14-30 (NLT - Parable of the Talents)—Again, the Kingdom of Heaven can be illustrated by the story of a man going on a long trip. He called together his servants and entrusted his money to them while he was gone. He gave five bags of silver to one, two bags of silver to another, and one bag of silver to the last—dividing it in proportion to their abilities. He then left on his trip.

"The servant who received the five bags of silver began to invest the money and earned five more. The servant with two bags of silver also went to work and earned two more. But the servant who received the one bag of silver dug a hole in the ground and hid the master's money.

"After a long time their master returned from his trip and called them to give an account of how they had used his money. The servant to whom he had entrusted the five bags of silver came forward with five more and said, 'Master, you gave me five bags of silver to invest, and I have earned five more.'

"The master was full of praise. 'Well done, my good and faithful servant. You have been faithful in handling this small amount, so now I will give you many more responsibilities. Let's celebrate together! "The servant who had received the two bags of silver came forward and said, 'Master, you gave me two bags of silver to invest, and I have earned two more.'

"The master said, 'Well done, my good and faithful servant. You have been faithful in handling this small amount, so now I will give you many more responsibilities. Let's celebrate together!'

"Then the servant with the one bag of silver came and said, 'Master, I knew you were a harsh man, harvesting crops you didn't plant and gathering crops you didn't cultivate. I was afraid I would lose your money, so I hid it in the earth. Look, here is your money back.'

"But the master replied, 'You wicked and lazy servant! If you knew I harvested crops I didn't plant and gathered crops I didn't cultivate, why didn't you deposit my money in the bank? At least I could have gotten some interest on it.'"Then he ordered, 'Take the money from this servant, and give it to the one with the ten bags of silver. To those who use well what they are given, even more will be given, and they will have an abundance. But from those who do nothing, even what little they have will be taken away. Now throw this useless servant into outer darkness, where there will be weeping and gnashing of teeth.'

Luke 12:13-21 *(NIV - Parable of the Rich Fool)—Someone in the crowd said to him, "Teacher, tell my brother to divide the inheritance with me." Jesus replied, "Man, who appointed me a judge or an arbiter between you?" Then he said to them, "Watch out! Be on your guard against all kinds of greed; life does not consist in an abundance of possessions." And he told them this parable: "The ground of a certain rich man yielded an abundant harvest. He thought to himself, 'What shall I do? I have no place to store my crops.' "Then he said, 'This is what I'll do. I will tear down my barns and build bigger ones, and there I will store my surplus grain. And I'll say to myself, "You have plenty of grain laid up for many years. Take life easy; eat, drink and be merry."' "But God said to him, 'You fool! This very night your life will be demanded from you. Then who will get what you have prepared for yourself?' "This is how it will be with whoever stores up things for themselves but is not rich toward God."*

🔒 **WISDOM KEY:**

Money doesn't change who you are; it simply emphasizes who you already were.

You may have heard someone say the phrase, "Money really changed that person." While it sounds correct when you initially hear it, the phrase itself is not true. Money is an inanimate object. Money is not good or bad. Money is a means to an end, and the person who holds the money decides whether it is good or bad.

Money is no different than a hammer. A hammer is an inanimate object that could be used to build a home for a single mom (good) or used as a murder weapon (bad). The only difference is how a person chooses to use the tool in their hand. You need to have a crystal-clear picture of your goals and dreams so you can strategically use every dollar that comes your way and properly steward and invest every dollar to achieve your goals. Money is simply a tool, and you get to decide whether that tool HELPS you achieve your goals or HURTS you in creating wealth.

As this book comes to an end, my hope is that you can think about your finances differently and properly steward and invest every dollar that comes your way. You have goals and dreams unique to you and your family, and only you can be the one to pursue those dreams. Your dreams deserve to be accomplished, and only you can be the one to achieve those dreams. Don't wait any longer. Get started today. A good plan in action is better than a perfect plan on paper.

Just because God put money in your hands doesn't mean He intends for it to stay there. More income won't make you a better steward. More income simply reveals who you already are. Get a clear picture of the vision you want for your future and go after it. Your family deserves it, your church deserves it, your community deserves it, and you deserve it. One dollar at a time and one "green light" choice at a time … go develop wealth to bless the world around you.

APPENDIX

Driving Instructions for Your Green Light Millionaire Journey

When you take a trip, make sure you follow the correct turns or else your trip takes longer than expected. The same is true with your financial journey. Make sure you don't get too far down the checklist before completing the initial turns on your journey. While your journey can vary depending on goals, be sure to start at the top and work your way down.

Pre-Trip Checklist

- **Goal List:** Have a clear picture of where you want to go.
- **Budget:** Know where each dollar goes every month.
- Invest in yourself the entire journey. You are your greatest asset.

Red Light Checklist

- **Emergency Savings:** Save $1,000 (protect against smaller short-term setbacks).
- **Debt:** Pay off all non-mortgage debt.
- **Emergency Fund:** three to six months expenses (protect against bigger setbacks).

Yellow Light Checklist

- Save 20 percent for a down-payment.
- Get a 15-year mortgage.
- Mortgage payment at 25 percent of net monthly income.

Green Light Checklist

Goal - invest 15 percent (or more) of your income toward retirement and long-term goals.

- Get the full match from your employer plan.
- Max out your own Roth IRA (if applicable).
- Increase your percentage into the employer plan until maxed out.
- Invest in a "wealth accumulation fund" to build wealth for your goals. This could be a brokerage account, real estate, or your own business and should be designed to help you achieve a goal on your list (generosity, retirement, kids' college, second home, travel, etc.).

Wisdom Key Summary

Chapter 2

- Let your assets pay for your liabilities.
- All assets should be connected with a specific goal.
- Things that last typically aren't built fast.

Chapter 3

- It's not how much you make, it's how much you keep.
- You can't get to your long-term goals with your parking brake on.
- Have an account just for "fun" for you and your family.

Chapter 4

- Your home is not a financial asset.

Chapter 5

- Assets should travel at the speed of your goals.
- Taxes are Uncle Sam's friend, not yours.

Chapter 6

- Find the goal underneath the goal, and clarify it as much as possible.
- Have a goal that will outlive you and bless those around you.
- Comparison is the root of all unhappiness.

Chapter 7

- Track net worth annually to provide guidance on your progress.
- Compounding interest is king.

Chapter 8

- Never take advice from someone who doesn't have what you want.
- The best investment you can make … is in yourself.

Chapter 9

- Stewardship never ends; it's a lifelong pursuit.
- Pass on financial wisdom, not just financial wealth.
- Money doesn't change who you are, it simply emphasizes who you already were.

Bonus

WISDOM KEYS AND QUOTES FOR YOUR FINANCIAL JOURNEY

- Good thinking precedes good results.
- People who are winning financially know a rising tide raises all ships, so they aren't concerned when they see other people building wealth.
- How much you make isn't nearly as important as what you do with it.
- The road to success is always under construction.
- What you resist persists.
- Money is like a rope. You can use it as a tool to pull you closer to your goals or tie it into a noose to hang yourself financially.
- It's easier to maintain good financial health than to regain it.
- Wealth is blind, it doesn't care if you have a master's degree or are a high school dropout.
- Successful people make the major decisions in their life right away and manage them daily.
- A wise person does first what a fool does last. Both do the same thing; only at different times.
- You are only as good as your worst habit. (Example - You don't spend much on eating out, but spend tons on clothing.)
- If you don't have a plan, more money will only bring you more problems.

- Don't be afraid to make yourself a priority. (Put money aside for your future self.)
- Money is an ally or an enemy...you choose with every dollar you send out that will either fight for your goals or against your goals.
- It's not a money problem; it's a behavior problem.
- The best way to judge future behavior is to investigate past behavior.
- The mind is like a parachute; it works better when it is open. (Always be teachable.)
- No matter how wealthy you become, you'll always be one bad decision away from going backward.
- Your money is an extension of yourself.
- Don't save what is left after spending, but spend what is left after saving.
- A small leak will sink a great ship. (Beware of little expenses.)
- Rich people stay rich living like they're broke. Broke people stay broke by living like they're rich.
- The more you learn, the more you can earn.
- Don't work for money. Make money work for you.
- You can't save your way to wealth; you have to invest to get there.
- Wealth is not about having a lot of money; it's about having a lot of options.
- Investing is about multiplying, not just maintaining.
- How you manage money directly reflects your values.
- Money doesn't solve problems - it exposes your discipline.
- Most people go broke trying to look rich.
- God gave you a seed, not a couch. Stop sitting on it.
- If your financial plan doesn't honor God, it's already broken.

Other Recommended Books

- *Total Money Makeover* by Dave Ramsey
- *Cashflow Quadrant* by Robert Kiyosaki
- *Millionaire Next Door* by Thomas Stanley
- *The Next Millionaire Next Door* by Thomas Stanley and Sarah Stanley Fallaw
- *God and Money* by John Cortines and Gregory Baumer
- *Start With Why* by Simon Sinek (Goal setting)

References

PREFACE

1. Thomas Carlyle, *On Heroes, Hero-Worship, and the Heroic in History* (London: James Fraser, 1841), Lecture V, "The Hero as Man of Letters."

CHAPTER 6

1. Kelly McGonigal, *The Upside of Stress: Why Stress Is Good for You, and How to Get Good at It* (New York: Avery, 2015), 146.
2. https://www.facebook.com/share/p/17N69hExZY/
3. Stanley, Andy. *The Principle of the Path.* Thomas Nelson, 2009, p. 14.

CHAPTER 7

1. *The Office*, season 3, episode 16, "Business School," directed by Joss Whedon, written by Brent Forrester, aired February 15, 2007, on NBC.

CHAPTER 8

1. https://corporate.vanguard.com/content/corporate-site/us/en/corp/articles/quantifying-evolution-advice-and-value-investors.html

ABOUT THE AUTHOR

Dave is a Senior Partner at Meadowland Financial Group which is a top Wealth Management Group in the Midwest. Prior to being an advisor and joining Meadowland Financial Group Dave was a pastor for 9 years and had a passion for helping people. He still has that same passion today with financial conversations being the front door that's used to build relationships with others to help them achieve their goals. Financial planning can get complex at times and Dave loves taking complex situations and simplifying those topics for his clients which was the premise of this book. Dave works with millionaires on a constant basis. Many times their clients goals are to pass down their wealth to the next generation ensuring proper stewardship to kids and grand-kids. By creating simple visual analogies Dave helps clients enjoy their retirement years while feeling empowered to bless others around them. When he's not assisting clients you will find Dave spending time with his wife Jackie and their kids Ethan and Emma while being active outdoors and serving in various capacities in their community.

Dave DeVries, CFP®, CKA®, RICP®, MDiv
www.greenlightmillionaire.com
www.linkedin.com/in/davejdevries
www.facebook.com/davejdevries

ABOUT THE COMPANY

Meadowland Financial Group is one of the top wealth management groups in the Midwest while working with clients all around the country. As a team they have received the Forbes Best In State Wealth Management Teams in 2024 and have been voted Local Best multiple years in a row. Their commitment to building lasting relationships and delivering tailored solutions sets them apart in the financial industry. Their clients benefit from a highly collaborative team of seasoned professionals, each with a deep understanding of financial planning and a dedication to achieving lasting results. At Meadowland Financial Group, they don't just manage wealth; they help you build a legacy. All their advisors hold the prestigious CERTIFIED FINANCIAL PLANNER™ (CFP®) designation. This certification is a mark of our advisors' expertise, ethical commitment, and dedication to delivering superior financial advice. Whether you are an individual seeking to grow and protect your wealth, or an institution in need of strategic financial guidance, Meadowland Financial Group stands ready to provide the expertise, insight, and personalized care you deserve.

Dave DeVries
7505 S. Louise Ave.
Sioux Falls, SD 57103
605-371-2258
www.meadowlandfinancialgroup.com/team/dave-devries-cfp-cka-ricp

ACKNOWLEDGEMENTS

To my wife, thanks for putting up with me and all the dreams I continue to chase. To my kids, thanks for being a sounding board to help me make ideas as simple as possible. To my parents, I have learned more from you about finances, relationships, and leadership than you will ever know. To all those who gave input into this book and have cheered me on, thanks for the encouragement and feedback to help make me (and this book) the best version possible. To God, thank you for my wife, kids, family and friends. Everything I have (including my finances) is from you. May the words in these pages be used to honor you in every way, shape and form.

ENDORSEMENTS CONTINUED

Green Light Millionaire *is a unique take on a familiar topic. Dave provides a clear, practical, and encouraging guide that shows everyday people how to build lasting wealth. This book helps you rethink money in ways that can change your family's future. If you want a roadmap to financial freedom that really works, this is it.*

– Billy Wilson,
Mountain Plains District Superintendent, The Wesleyan Church

Green Light Millionaire *is a practical guide that shows how everyday people can build lasting wealth by thinking differently about money. Dave combines real-life wisdom with clear principles that anyone can apply, making financial freedom both approachable and inspiring.*

– Joe Evenson,
President, Kingdom Capital Fund

Green Light Millionaire *isn't another get-rich-quick gimmick— it's a blueprint for building real, lasting wealth. Dave strips away the noise, teaching timeless financial principles through relatable stories and a simple but powerful framework. Whether you're starting out or starting over, this book will change how you think about money—and how you use it. Read it, apply it, and watch your green lights multiply.*

– Vince Miller,
Author & Speaker, Founder of Resolute

I have known Dave for over 25 years and if I had to describe him in one word, it would be disciplined - and this book is a great example of that! Through engaging content, practical advice, and stories that create understanding, Dave has written an easy-to-read resource that will help readers become more disciplined in managing and stewarding their finances, setting and reaching their goals, and living a fulfilling and God-honoring life. I have no doubt that Green Light Millionaire *will be a game changer for anyone who reads it.*

– Tom Henderson,
ResGen Founder, Speaker and Author

This book is a definite must-read for anyone who wants to learn how to get ahead. Dave provides simple steps that anyone can follow to achieve financial success. His genuine and approachable style makes the guidance feel personal, like a conversation with a close friend.

– Jayna Voss,
Co-Founder and Attorney, Legacy Law Firm, P.C.

I have known Dave for more than 25 years, and throughout that time I have witnessed his life marked by integrity, wisdom, and a genuine desire to help others flourish. In this book, he brings that same character and clarity to the topic of financial management. This is not just another book on money—it's a trustworthy resource from someone whose life matches his message.

– Jay Woudstra,
Superintendent, Sioux Falls Christian School

Green Light Millionaire *presents a thoughtful, practical and useful approach to personal finance and building financial security. The red light – green light approach provides the reader with a simple construct that can be used when making ordinary and extraordinary financial decisions. The simple traffic light construct allows the reader to take away real life skills that, if applied consistently, will undoubtedly lead to financial security.*

– Matt Tobin,
President/COO - South Dakota Trust Company LLC

In a world overflowing with financial noise and quick-fix prom-ises, Green Light Millionaire *stands out as a roadmap for real, sustainable wealth. This isn't about chasing the next hustle or trend, it's about understanding money with clarity and purpose. If you're ready to move beyond the grind and start building last-ing prosperity on your own terms, this book gives you the green light to go all in.*

– Josh Kattenberg,
Owner, Real Property Management Express

Dave offers us fresh and practical advice on making and manag-ing our wealth that is rooted in historical and biblical wisdom. Thank you, Dave, for helping a new generation live prosperously and generously to fulfill our purpose and calling in this life.

– Rev. Roger Spahr,
Former District Superintendent,
Dakotas District of the United Methodist Church

Green Light Millionaire *is an absolute must read — especially for young people who want to wisely navigate through the maze of financial decisions they will face. It will be mandatory reading for all of the young leaders coming into our organization. It's a realistic, thoughtful guide to financial freedom.*

– Rev. Wesley Smith,
District Superintendent of Northwest District,
The Wesleyan Church

I invite you to consider leaving traditional financial advice behind and read Green Light Millionaire. *This isn't just a book about money; it's a practical guide to the good life, thoughtfully weaving together financial strategies with biblical wisdom. Dave challenges us to see wealth not as something we merely accumu-late, but as a powerful tool for stewardship and generosity. For anyone striving to grow their wealth and leave a meaningful and lasting legacy, this book offers a profound and practical path.*

– Reed Sheard, Ed.D,
Vice President and Chief Information Officer, Westmont College

As a coach, I've stressed the importance of simplicity for our players so they can execute to the best of their abilities. This book follows those same principles that will help you understand and transform your thinking when it comes managing your finances. Dave is someone of high character and heavily studied in the area of finance and you will only stand to benefit by applying the strategies outlined in this book.

– Jed Stugart,
Head Football Coach, Lindenwood University

This book is an excellent guide for anyone looking to strengthen their financial knowledge. The author breaks down complex concepts into clear, practical advice that's easy to apply in real life. It's not only informative but also motivating, encouraging readers to take control of their money and build lasting wealth. A must-read for anyone serious about improving their financial future.

– Pat Azzara,
Co-Owner, Azzara Tax Services

I appreciate the pastoral heart Dave brings to this topic and the emphasis he places on stewarding that which God has entrusted to us. Dave makes it clear that doing so is both a responsibility and a gift.

– Greg Henson,
President, Kairos University

Green Light Millionaire *gets past the superficial goals of becoming wealthy and to the heart of the matter: Financial planning as a stewardship of God's gracious gifts. The presentation is accessible, and something I would encourage my kids to read as they become more responsible for their own financial position.*

– Rev. Dr. Wade Mobley,
President, Free Lutheran Bible College and Seminary

Green Light Millionaire *breaks down complex financial concepts into empowering, relatable lessons. Whether you're just starting out or looking to grow, this book will give you the confidence and exact road map to go after your financial goals.*

– Sarah Kurtenbach,
Founder, moveHER Money

Packed with lots of real-life scenarios, Dave offers both traditional and unconventional wisdom broken down into accessible concepts to help you analyze how you think about money and how to apply ultimate prudence to your personal finances. Building wealth truly is a mindset, and following the wisdom in these chapters is foundational for changing the financial future for you, your family, and your entire lineage!

– Kristi Jones,
Attorney at Law, Dakota Law Firm

Dave is someone who advises and leads with honesty, hard work, and a genuine desire to help people succeed. Green Light Millionaire *reflects his practical wisdom and ability to simplify complex financial principles into everyday decisions that truly make a difference. His sound advice and clear strategies make this a trustworthy guide for anyone serious about building lasting wealth.*

– Tyler Goff,
Founder, Team Leader at Tyler Goff Group

Many people miss out on financial independence because they misunderstand the fundamentals. Success isn't about earning more—it's about living below your means, saving and investing consistently. Too often, people assume wealth comes from high income or complicated strategies, when in truth, it's steady, disciplined habits over time that create lasting freedom. Dave breaks this down in simple terms, showing how to recognize and avoid life's "red lights" while focusing on the "green lights" that lead to long-term success.

– Todd Pharis,
Multi-Unit Owner of Pizza Ranch Restaurants and
Chairman of the Pizza Ranch Franchise Advisory Council

Any time I read a book I want to know that the author has the following qualities - pure intent, genuine humility, professional experience, emits practicality vs. theory and creates a memorable framework. Dave DeVries exhibits all these attributes and more. His truth telling and green light, red light guide posts create a life changing journey for any reader brave enough to start making changes now. Dig in! Your future self will thank you.

– Tim Schmidt,
Executive Coach, International Speaker,
Founder of DRYDOCK Consulting LLC,
Author, *What Really Works - the 7Fs - Faith | Family | Finances | Fitness | Friends | Fun | Future*

Green Light Millionaire *is a clear and insightful quick read. This book highlights how small, consistent financial decisions can have massive compounding effects over time. Find the approach that fits for you and let time do the rest!*

– Bryan Hakeman,
Owner, Dakota CPA

The fable of Joe Wealthy and Ben Broke, along with the Red Light vs. Green Light analogy, made it fun to read and easy to understand. It's a smart, simple way to help people rethink how they handle money.

– Nick Ovenden,
President, GreatLIFE

Green Light Millionaire *offers a refreshingly down-to-earth approach to personal finance that empowers its readers with actionable advice to build wealth and achieve financial independence.*

– Evan Anema,
Partner and Attorney at Law, Estate Planning Solutions

Are you interested in becoming a millionaire? The path to wealth and leaving a financial legacy for our families may seem daunting and unattainable. In Green Light Millionaire, *Dave de-mystifies the steps to becoming a millionaire. This practical guide is for everyone—from age 18 to 88. If you want to know this strategy, this easy-to-read book will give you the roadmap.*

– Linda P. Outka,
Leadership Coach and Author of *Pebbles in My Shoe: Three Steps to Breaking through Interpersonal Conflict*

Dave draws upon his unique life experiences to empower families as they prepare for their futures. It is truly inspiring to see how he integrates these principles into the complex world of financial planning. When it comes to securing your family's economic well-being, you could not place your trust in more capable hands. This book captures the idea that financial planning can occur without sacrificing Christian ethics, offering a refreshing and unique perspective.

– Cody Bozied,
Owner/Operator - Napa Auto Parts

It doesn't matter how old you are, what you have or who you are, Green Light Millionaire *will give you a framework and gameplan on how to achieve your financial goals. Dave has lived this out in his personal life, and now can help you live it out as well.*

– Reed DeVries,
Pastor, Business Owner

Practical wisdom meets powerful storytelling. Green Light Millionaire *is not just about money—it's about mindset and the discipline that leads to financial freedom. From red-light mistakes to green-light opportunities, this book maps the journey to wealth creation in a way that's easy to follow and impossible to ignore.*

– Tony Nour,
Senior Vice President,
Relationship Banking - First PREMIER Bank

I've personally seen Dave faithfully live out the very principles of this book — choosing green lights that build lasting wealth and freedom, while steering clear of the red lights that can derail so many. Because he doesn't just teach these ideas but embodies them, I can wholeheartedly endorse both Dave and the powerful message of Green Light Millionaire.

– Rob Fagnan, SIOR,
Principal at Bender Commercial Real Estate Services

Green Light Millionaire *is one of the most practical books on wealth-building I've ever read. Dave doesn't just inspire, he gives you clear, actionable steps you can actually follow. If you apply what he lays out and avoid the common pitfalls he warns against, you will become a millionaire, it's that straightforward. This is a must-read for anyone ready to take control of their financial future.*

– Travis Finke,
Executive Pastor, Embrace Church

This book should be required reading. Straightforward, practical financial advice from a man who walks the walk every day. I will be recommending this book to all my clients.

– Kevin Carlson,
Senior Mortgage Banker, Plains Commerce Bank

I promise you from personal experience, the principles Dave teaches in this book really work, and they work across the spectrum of income ranges. You don't need to have a six figure income to become a Green Light Millionaire. *Read this book to find out why.*

– Galen Ensz,
CPA

I've known Dave as a friend for over 25 years and he's always had a gift for stewarding finances. In Green Light Millionaire, *he makes his years of experience and training accessible to everyone with easy to grasp concepts and engaging stories. This book is going to bless lots of people!*

– Dave Sinkgraven,
Senior Pastor, Life Church

Green Light Millionaire *is a fresh, visual, and grounded approach to personal finance that's accessible for all generations. Dave bridges timeless Biblical wisdom with practical tools to help families steward their wealth with clarity and purpose.*

– Kyle Schull,
President & CEO, Building Products Inc.

Dave isn't just someone who teaches about wealth, he's someone who has lived it. From pastoral ministry to financial advising, he's walked the road of financial wisdom with integrity, humility, and results. What makes this book so impactful is that it doesn't sell hype or shortcuts, it offers clarity, perspective, and practical tools to help everyday people think differently and win with money. Green Light Millionaire *is relatable, visual, and refreshingly honest. Whether you're just starting your journey or looking to take your next step, Dave will help you shift your mindset and take meaningful action.*

– Tim Troxell,
Lead Pastor, Generations Church

In this insightful book, my friend and ministry partner brings a fresh perspective to financial practices through the simple yet powerful stoplight analogy. This framework speaks to people at every stage of their financial journey. Grounded in biblical truth and community, the book moves beyond wealth creation to inspire faithful stewardship that leads to lasting impact.

– Nate Helling,
Executive Vice President and
Chief Financial Officer, Kairos University

I can think of no other person than Dave that has the authority to teach about discipline, especially with money. He practices what he preaches, and I have decades of experiences with him to prove it. Read this book if you want tried and true lessons on building wealth!

– Chris Haugan,
Former Pastor and current Mortgage Banker

Dave breaks down the different paths of life's financial journey in a way that anyone can understand. He provides easy-to-digest, real-world examples that both teach and serve as helpful reminders for people at any stage of that journey.

— **Rocky Welker,**
Executive Director, Habitat For Humanity of Greater Sioux Falls

Dave does an impressive job simplifying oftentimes complex financial matters. For most Americans, finances are front of mind every single day. For a lot of Americans, so are traffic lights! What a great daily reminder to reinforce the messaging in this book.

– **Peter Siegling,**
Managing Partner, Meadowland Financial Group

In reading this book I see many principles from scripture on how to succeed financially. I wish I would have had his book and applied myself to these principles many years ago, instead of learning them the hard way.

– **Mike Nichols,**
Nichols Marketing Solutions

Green Light Millionaire *is a gamechanger! Dave unpacks timeless financial wisdom through his red, yellow, and green light framework, making it easy for anyone to understand and apply. The sooner you put these principles into practice, the sooner your life will change. Green means go—so go get this book!*

– **Monte Gannon,**
Lead Pastor, Meadows Church

I trust Dave not just when it comes to money, but in the way he lives his life with faith and integrity. Green Light Millionaire *is full of down-to-earth advice that actually works, showing how to make smart choices that honor God and grow your wealth. This book is a simple, practical guide for anyone who wants to get their finances in order and reach their goals.*

– **Dr. Nate DeJong,**
Founder/Owner, Highest Health Chiropractic and
Owner, Mission Properties and Owner, Freedom South Dakota

Dave does an incredible job of breaking down the complex topic of finances and wealth-building into easy-to-follow, actionable steps toward financial independence. Whether you're an experienced investor or just starting your journey, Green Light Millionaire *is one of the best books available to support the process and provide practical guidance for building wealth. A must-read for anyone exploring the world of investing or finance.*

– Matthew Stange,
Managing Partner, Meadowland Financial Group

Dave is a principled, and trustworthy business professional. His simple to read book is an easy to understand formula to gain and maintain wealth in today's complex world.

– Scott Riley,
Business Owner

There are so many financial principles in this – if applied - can make a significant difference in the future of you and your family. It is definitely worth the read!!

– Cindy DeVries,
Business Owner

Green Light Millionaire *completely shifted my perspective on wealth. It's not just about chasing the latest hot investments; it's about making smart money moves that truly build your future. Using practical concepts, this book helps you take control of your finances and make everyday choices that actually create lasting wealth. If you're ready to truly understand money, grow your finances, and live a life with real purpose, you need to read this book!*

– Brian Rock,
57th Street Campus Pastor, Embrace Church

Dave's book provides both solid and wise principles to build your future wealth on. A key takeaway is having the right financial mindset to build good habits that will impact your family legacy!

– Jim Rieffenberger,
Coach/Mentor

Dave put together a fantastic book on becoming financially successful. It brings together very simple but powerful ideas on common sense ways to set one's self up for reaching their personal goals. My favorite topic was don't compare yourselves to others. If you follow the general principles in this book you will have a "Green Light" for financial freedom.

– Ryan Spellerberg,
25 year mortgage banker and current
Sioux Falls City Council member

A powerful source of positivity and energy, Dave delivers sound high level financial strategies while at the same time doing it in a Christian way. A must read for both the beginner and expert investor.

– Ross McDaniel, DC,
Founder of ChiroSport, PC

This isn't another cookie-cutter financial book, it's a clear, practical, and relatable roadmap to building lasting wealth. Dave's "Green Light / Red Light" framework will forever change the way you think about money, and his principles work no matter what your income level is. If you want to think differently, live wisely, and create a lasting legacy that matters, Green Light Millionaire *is a must-read.*

– Austin Walker,
Lead Pastor at Embrace Church (MN),
Founder and President of Apex Gathering

Green Light Millionaire *flips the script on wealth-building. It's not about chasing money, it's about mastering the way you think about it. This book is a game-changer for anyone ready to rewrite their financial future.*

– Marcus Squier,
President & CEO, Paulsen

www.ingramcontent.com/pod-product-compliance
Lightning Source LLC
Chambersburg PA
CBHW050509210326
41521CB00011B/2388